mum's
cooking
for **lads** away from **home**

text dominique ayral
illustrations jean-pierre cagnat

fitway.
publishing

in the same series

trainers, sandrine pereira

underdressed, élodie piveteau – philippe vaurès santamaria

men's watches, hervé borne

© Fitway Publishing, 2005
Original editions in French, English, Spanish, Italian

All rights reserved, including partial or complete translation, adaptation and
reproduction rights, in any form and for any purpose

Translation by Translate-A-Book, Oxford
Design and creation: GRAPH'M/Nord Compo, France

ISBN: 2-7528-0199-8
Publisher code: T00199

Copyright registration: October 2005
Printed in Italy by Rotolito Lombarda

www.fitwaypublishing.com

Fitway Publishing
12, avenue d'Italie – 75627 Paris cedex 13, France

I dedicate this notebook of recipes to you, my son.

It's a sort of travel log, where I have recorded my stories.

Now it's your turn to write yours. Create your own universe,

invent a way of cooking that belongs to you.

Cook the classic dishes, cook the modern ones,

mix the two. Do as you please.

With my love,   *Mum*

Notes

Standard level spoon measurements are used in all recipes.

I tablespoon = one 15 ml spoon

I teaspoon = one 5 ml spoon

Both metric and imperial measurements have been given in all recipes. Use one set of measurements only and not a mixture of both.

The Department of Health advises that eggs should not be consumed raw. This book contains dishes made with raw or lightly cooked eggs. It is prudent for any vulnerable people to avoid uncooked or lightly cooked dishes made with eggs. Once prepared these dishes should be kept refrigerated and used promptly.

This book includes dishes made with nuts and nut derivatives. It is advisable for readers with known allergic reactions to nuts and nut derivatives, and those who may be potentially vulnerable to these allergies, to avoid dishes made with nuts and nut oils. It is also prudent to check the labels of pre-prepared ingredients for the possible inclusion of nut derivatives.

for you, MY SON

You came down this morning, with your suitcase all packed. I was sitting in the kitchen, near the window. You said, 'Don't worry, Mum, I'll be coming back'. It gave me a funny feeling; a lump came to my throat. My whispered reply betrayed a mother's fears when her child is on the point of leaving home: 'Yes, but only as a traveller passing through – stopping at the nearest hotel and scarcely unpacking your luggage, so there'll be no way of knowing whether you've just arrived or are about to be off again'.

You're embarking on a long journey to be a student many miles away. Where will your first job take you? Where will your loves lead you? Life is claiming you, beckoning you on with its unknown paths and countless possibilities, numerous as the lines on a hand. It's time to stand on your own two feet now – I won't hold you back. I set to, cooking furiously as for a feast. Go and fetch your grandmother. Your father will soon be here. We're going to send the traveller off in style.

From now on, home will be a staging post or resting place where you can always find food and shelter and go off again, stocked up with supplies.

I'm giving you an assortment of starters for the journey and for settling into your new home: *hummus, tzatziki, roasted peppers, chouchouka, bruschetta, ricotta with mixed herbs, cannellini bean salad with thyme and basil, chicken liver pâté* … They're Mediterranean recipes, specialities of Spain, Italy, Greece, Turkey and Lebanon. Tapas, antipasti or mezze – enjoy them all, my son. Your roots are still here.

When I cook, I don't follow the recipes in books to the letter. I skim through them to get a general idea, and then I invent. That's how I see cooking – with a degree of freedom to do what you want. If I need inspiration I look at a comic (yes, a strip cartoon), a serious newspaper (there's always a lighter, more escapist section), an art magazine showing pictures and sculptures, or a novel. It doesn't matter what, as long as I am entertained.

I gave myself a day to get used to your not being here. But now I'm on edge. Since this morning I haven't stopped reading Edith Wharton's *In Morocco*, and it's as if I'm in that country in the summer of 1917. I am a Westerner exploring territory that is still unknown. I shelter for a few moments in the shade of an aged fig tree clamped in uptorn tiles. I go off towards the secret pool to which childless women are brought to bathe. I walk through the terraced orange-garden. I see the bric-a-brac in the souk.

I am intoxicated by its noise, the smell of dates and the alcohol drunk by the men, by the smell of camels and spices, black bodies and smoking fry that hangs like a fog … I feel like making you some *couscous with dates and walnuts*. I'll sprinkle it with cinnamon and add some walnuts for decoration. Walnuts aren't really Moroccan but I like the idea. I like the combination of dates, walnuts and cinnamon with savoury couscous – sweet and sour with the dried fruits. It conjures up the vast desert.

Cooking is built on a dream. There are images scattered all around and what we do is assemble them to give pleasure to those we love.

The wind covers my skin with a film of dust and I am warmed by its ochre colour. I fancy a touch of orange. Do you remember my *orange salad*? I slice the oranges and scatter them with threads of saffron – bright orange against the setting sun. The beauty of unexpected flavours and tones of colour set side by side. I pour some drops of green olive oil over the salad. The sweet acidity of the orange and the bitter sweetness of the pressed olive juice pervade me. The saffron has such a particular pungency. Let's continue to aim for the dramatic effect while indulging our gourmandise. How many times have you looked longingly at my *poached pears with saffron and vanilla syrup?* Black vanilla seeds and the same bright orange saffron, two colours crushed together and sprinkled over the round contours of the pale yellow pears. Will I ever get used to the idea of your going? As a last desperate hope, I create another spicy and sweetly-flavoured work of art.

I look at my *apples bonne femme*, hollowed out and filled with raisins and slivers of almonds, honey, cinnamon and lemon peel. I can't keep you to myself any longer.

I remember the summer of 1999. I can just see you as you were then – our fifteen-year-old son. We'd taken you on holiday to Morocco. We knew, your father and I, that it would be our last family trip for a long time. In future you would spend your holidays with your friends. We had agreed on this arrangement so as to have you with us for the days that remained. In this race against time, we became dizzy with visits and heady scents. Away from the dark, narrow streets, we were showered by the explosion of colours and we feasted on the hot, abundant food. What a treat it was to feel you responding. For the first time, you were affected by food. Normally you hated carrots, but there you loved them – your only hesitation was whether to eat them raw or cooked. Faced with a choice between *carrot and almond salad* and *carrot and green olive salad*, you managed somehow to take both, 'because of the flavour of the spices,' you explained. It made us laugh.

We would eat however we could, perched at the end of a table or sometimes standing up. It was much more relaxed and informal than at home. You laughed and made fun of us, demanding plates of olives – black, green, spiced, or with candied lemon. You wanted to touch everything, taste everything. You became a small child again, full of mischief at the sight of the funny terracotta dishes with their conical covers. There was a surprise waiting inside, like in the magician's hat. Besides, 'it smelled good,' you pronounced, licking your lips. In one dish was chicken with green olives, in the other meat balls. Some were overflowing with aubergines, others with lamb. They were all called 'tagine' – you liked that name. You adopted it as part of your vocabulary instead of using 'stew': 'It sounded much nicer.'

The charm of this bit of North Africa enveloped you in its soft caress. You opened up to the world. We were happy. So that you don't lose sight of that moment as you leave us and start to travel, I'm giving you a tagine dish. Put it in the luggage for your journey. It's big enough for six people.

They do come smaller than that and there are others that are bigger, more impressive. This one comes from Fez. We brought it back from our holiday together. I guarded it jealously, like a full cup to be offered up when the time came. You'll find it useful for the long stopovers at your new address.

You cook things slowly – or braise them – in a tagine. You can put it directly over a low heat, either an electric ring or a gas flame. It will also go in the oven. Prepare tagines of chicken with olives and meat balls. But don't stop there. Play at being an alchemist. Invent. You'll see, as you gain more experience, that you can do almost anything with a tagine dish ; it's very versatile. If you break it, no need to panic. You can always find another way of cooking.

I've also given you a cooking pot, in which you can do all sorts. Like the tagine, it will cook and simmer meat or vege-table stews, but you can boil things in it as well. Then there's a frying pan for frying and browning, or searing meat.

You can simmer food in a frying pan too, over a low heat. I've put in a cake tin, for making sweet or savoury cakes,

custards, desserts or pâtés; and then a roasting dish to be used in the oven, for roasting meat and vegetables. If you put a little water in the bottom, it can serve as a bain-marie. I've given you three saucepans of different sizes for boiling, cooking and reheating, and a pie dish. You can gradually add to your equipment. An electric food mixer or handheld blender is handy for liquidising fruit and vegetables.

If you want, I'll buy you a wok for your birthday. It's really great to be able to cook, fry, seal and simmer all in the same large pan with its rounded base. Then I've given you a large bowl that will be handy for preparing salads, but also for mixing ingredients, or whisking eggs or marinating raw meat. I use a bowl like that for assembling all the ingredients for *steak tartare*.

The method I use for making *steak tartare* comes from my own student days. I got it from Monsieur Henri, a waiter at the Deux G brasserie, where I used to hang out before and after lectures. And especially during, which is the best time for discovering life. I became one of the gang who made it their home, becoming firm friends along the way. Imagination and unwillingness to conform were what drew us together, and we all shared the same determination to devour life. But what a tough creature it was! Our nights spent chasing after it left us feeling shattered. Christian, your godfather, decided that a daily serving of steak tartare was what was needed to perk us up. The raw meat, well seasoned with a strong sauce, would soon see us ready for the attack again. Avid as we were for sensations, it would be a perfect match for our wild existence.

Christian's talk mesmerised us; his attitude had us all eating out of his hand. He had a knack of always managing somehow to occupy the same bit of bench, at the pivotal point between indoors and out, separated by the solid transparency of the glass window. He would pretend to have his head buried in a newspaper and, from his vantage point, he would observe everything.

All the gang was there, late on Friday afternoon, holding court at the hour for enjoying a steaming cup of tea. Christian stood up, an imposing figure with his fine moustache. 'Monsieur Henri makes the best steak tartare in the Deux G,' he announced. We had never known Christian look so serious (so much so that he had lost his lilting accent), and we were plunged into silence. A passing waiter, used to our rowdiness, asked if everything was all right. It was a solemn moment. Why had we not yet tasted Monsieur Henri's steak tartare? We should put that right.

The next day, by one o'clock, we were all seated, fork in hand (no need for a knife), waiting for the attack. We would be impartial judges. We had ordered steak tartare from the brasserie menu several times before, without being particularly impressed. It had lacked that special something that makes all the difference. We were treading a fine line, ready to give up the quest – but willing to place our last hopes in Monsieur Henri. He was the one appointed to do the honours on Saturday lunchtimes.

Monsieur Henri set up a dumbwaiter at the end of our table, and laid out all the ingredients in their order of priority for creating of the dish. In a large bowl, he mixed together strong mustard, Worcestershire sauce®, Tabasco®, salt and lemon juice, then fresh egg yolks, which he broke in front of us. Pouring in a few drops of olive oil, he whisked hard and continuously. The thin trickle of olive oil made the smooth mixture swell and become shiny – almost as shiny as our eyes, which were popping out on stalks. At this point he added pepper, then parsley, capers and gherkins. He mixed one last time, lifting up the translucent blend.

It was ready. Its strength could now be measured against that of the deep crimson meat waiting, like tangled spaghetti, in another bowl.

Monsieur Henri spooned the tartare on to the plates, moulding it into the shape of minced steaks. Then he put one in front of each of us, together with some hot, crunchy chips, and wished us 'bon appétit'.

It was smooth and captivating in the mouth. Nothing clashed. Quite the opposite – by working up the sauce like a mayonnaise with seasoning, Monsieur Henri had captured all the flavours, and held them in the emulsified oil. On contact with the raw meat, they then simply exploded and unfurled, making a sensual assault on the taste buds. *That* was Monsieur Henri's secret. *That* was the difference from all the other steak tartares. Monsieur Henri had proved to us that the untamed and the civilised could co-exist. From that day on, the new strength we had acquired never left us. Monsieur Henri's steak tartare became our touchstone, and the man himself became our guiding star.

We all felt the same way – young as we were, we knew how to get round Monsieur Henri and he would spoil us every Saturday with his steak tartare. He also gave us cooking tips by the dozen. He said that cooking enabled you to be at one with existence. Food was Nature's sacred gift for living in harmony within civilisation. We should respect it. It was a form of love.

Christian, who didn't know what to do with his future, finally understood the meaning of his dalliance at the Deux G. In this place, classed as an Historic Monument, in this hall of mirrors where the reflected red seats emphasised the elegance of the waiters in their tails and black bow ties, he embraced his destiny in the way he embraced his women with their red lips.

From stolen kisses to apprenticeships with master chefs, Christian was never again to abandon either his cooking stove or the hearts of young ladies. Mad Pierrot that he was, reaching for the moon meant adding a 'Menu tomates' to his summer specialities. It was a sudden whim, 'after returning from a trip to Paris,' he said, without further explanation.

Try as I might to dig further on our yearly visit, when he presented us with the new dishes on his menu, Christian remained obdurate. Then, one evening, a couple of years ago, you were with us when he asked for our opinion of his tomato tartare. He was very proud of this dish: 'I've worked particularly hard on the flavour, to bring out the natural freshness associated with the word "tartare". It's also a tribute to Monsieur Henri,' he explained.

It was fresh and delicately flavoured. The chives and tangy olive oil titillated our taste buds, enhanced by the pungent basil with its suggestion of sun. The well-ripened tomato was sprinkled with drops of wonderfully aromatic balsamic vinegar. Pure nectar! Appetites sharpened and glasses filled with a wine of just the right temperature, Christian became more expansive and started to talk about his passion for the tomato. As the moments passed, he gradually recounted the story of that fateful November day in Paris. 'It was damp and grey. The sort of weather for collecting snails from wild fennel branches in the south of France, rather than freezing here… fresh and delicately flavoured.'

'I was annoyed. I'd caught the train to go and meet a pretty Mexican girl in the Place Saint-Michel. But she didn't turn up. I trailed around the streets, looking downcast and staring at the paving stones. I could see no further than my own misery and the blow to my ego. I had been stood up, set up for nothing – it was too much for one man to take. In my anger I bumped into a passer-by. After offering some lame excuse, I turned and headed off in another direction, which brought me face to face with a metre of full red lips spewing water into a pool. Diagonally behind them, a huge heart was turning, red on one side and green and orange on the other. Niki de Saint-Phalle's live sculptures brought me back to earth. Or perhaps there's another version of events? The bells of the neighbouring church were just striking midday. I automatically checked the time on my watch, which still showed eight o'clock. My lovely brunette must have found the wait too long and left.'

His moustache suddenly drooped. 'Didn't you phone her?' we all howled in chorus.

'I didn't dare. I was torn between pride and shame – how could I explain such a ridiculous story?'

Christian took the first train listed on the departures board at the station. And from that late autumn day until the first day of summer, he slaved away in the evenings after his restaurant had closed until he was able to display the fruits of his shame on the menu.

He went into battle with an army of greenhouse tomatoes (which tided him over until the tomato season arrived), concocting dozens and dozens of tomato recipes. These he wrote down with the emotion of a conquistador discovering the New World. Every night, alone in his kitchens, it was as if Christian were gathering the red fruits from the land of the Aztecs, those ancestors of his Mexican beauty, for the very first time. Every night he would discover their mysteries afresh. It was his way of seeking forgiveness.

Ever since the days of Monsieur Henri and with the wealth of experience gained by your godfather, Christian, I have believed in the idea that cooking breaks down barriers. I go from one civilisation to another; I jump from one continent to another. I am in the past, present and future. I am at the centre of the world of cooking; in the land of 'World Food', as the current expression has it. It is a universal language, uniting all the most delicious specialities on the planet.

Coleslaw, Caesar salad, spring rolls, salade niçoise, ratatouille, guacamole, prawn curry, tandoori chicken, chicken fajitas, chilli con carne, fish and chips, spaghetti bolognaise, penne carbonara, cheesecake, tiramisu, panna cotta with fruit coulis, brownies, rice pudding and pain perdu ... My head is turning with these comforting names. Thanks to them, I can travel without even moving from the house. I can surf from one recipe to another. I am borne along by their timelessness.

Their names and the basic methods for making them cannot go out of fashion. The rest I improvise, since there is
hardly anybody who still knows the original recipes. So
much the better – it means you can tell stories. True or
false, it doesn't matter. I want to be transported by these
recipes to another world, as one is by the stars of stage and
screen. With World Food, I can be a net surfer weaving
a spider's web in the cyberspace of the culinary universe.
Knit one, purl one, cooking is a game – con-
struction and deconstruction. I organise, I revisit
and I amalgamate, always accompanied by music.
I play at being a DJ as I stir the mixtures in my saucepans. I
move from classical to jazz as I watch the puff pastry of the
smoked salmon and fresh goat's cheese tart browning in the
oven. I steer a course between the counter-tenor of Vival-
di's *Stabat Mater* and the jazzy notes of the pianist Brad
Mehldau. Slices of cucumber, slices of smoked salmon,
wasabi cream – I come down to earth with a *millefeuille*
coloured green and orange, on the sway-
ing beats of the electronic music.

Using avocado and chilli powder, I turn the *Spanish gazpacho* into a *Mexican gazpacho*. Like the DJs in the Detroit clubs, I mix and remix. Cookery for grand occasions, world cookery, regional cookery, ethnic cookery, I reinterpret what I feel. I create an urban cuisine.

I exchange your grandmother's savoury olive cake for a sweet version of *cherry cake with candied lemon peel*. I'm counting on the surprise effect of my other sweet cake with grated carrot and flaked almonds. Doesn't that remind you of Morocco? I've turned the courgette custard that you found so dull into a *ricotta loaf with courgettes*. Will that give it a kick now, as you would say? One has to move with the times. I cook in the spirit of the age, bringing together unexpected ingredients and ways of cooking. I orchestrate mini-symphonies of flavours.

Pepper, chilli, Tabasco®, tandoori, soy sauce, cumin, paprika. I mustn't spoil the dish: I put in just the right amount. I leave the harissa and take my sardines in oil, resting on slices of toast, out of their pineapple, sundried tomato and pine nut dressing. I emerge from my culinary

trip to the accompaniment of Sarah Vaughan's *Lover Man*. Remixed, of course! Jazz is so delicious like that! Cooking is delicious, too – you just have to be daring and go off the beaten track. To a background mixture of rap and classical violins, I bring together Mexico, the farmyard and modern manufacturing methods. I start off on a sharp, quick rhythm with my sweetcorn *pancakes*. The *chicken kebabs* are crunchy with sesame seeds. Then comes the soothing softness of the *tofu* infusing in the coconut milk. This alternation of captivating rhythms is good. I abandon the *Spanish tortilla* for the crunchy crisps, crumbled up and sprinkled over a runny omelette.

I make fusion food, as it's called these days, while listening to The Streets. There's a drum roll in *It's too late*. No, it's never too late to regress: little pots of *Nutella®* *cream, dark chocolate truffles, poached pears with saffron and vanila syrup*.

More food is keeping warm in the cooking pot. I put on *Finding Beauty*, by Craig Armstrong, before the guests arrive. Zen. I remain zen. We'll eat in an hour's time,

with a little easy-listening music in the background. Will the atmosphere be oriental or Indian? Argentinian tunes, bossa nova or fado? Nothing is decided yet. Everything is still evolving. As with music, I like the idea that cooking advances. There is always something new to contemplate: another angle, another point of view. With that kind of rhythm, there's no chance of my being bored when cooking. I hope it will be the same for you.

Cooking is not difficult if you do it from the heart. That's the essence of good cooking – letting your heart speak; giving free rein to sensations; letting your senses awaken. You touch, feel, smell, look, listen, imagine. Cooking is a journey to the land of love.

Bon voyage, my son.

PS: Most of the recipes I've selected will cost less than £10. You can reheat some of them in the microwave: *ratatouille*, *pan of mixed vegetables*, coulis and sauces, and even *chouchouka*, as long as you cover the dish with cling-film suitable for use in the microwave.

have a go, it's

mum's cooking

dip for improvised pre-dinner nibbles

makes one bowl
preparation: 5 min
no cooking

1 tablespoon strong or seasoned mustard (or 1 teaspoon horseradish or wasabi)

250g/9 oz plain yogurt (or fromage frais)

1 tablespoon olive oil

3 drops Tabasco®

salt and pepper

Mix all the ingredients in a bowl.

Using this same base, you can make different dips with finely chopped herbs and seasonings, tomato purée or ketchup®, turmeric, lemon and dill, etc.

Serve with carrot or celery sticks, tacos, crisps, chunks of cheese – Gruyère, Emmenthal, Cheddar …

raïta

makes one bowl
preparation: 5 min
no cooking

1 cucumber

1 garlic clove

125g/4½ oz plain yogurt

salt and pepper

Wash and grate the cucumber. Peel and chop the garlic. Mix all the ingredients together.

talking of tomatoes

To peel tomatoes, make a cross with a knife where the stalk was and cover them with boiling water. Leave until the skins start to split. Drain the tomatoes and cover with cold water to stop them 'cooking' while you easily remove the skins. It is possible to peel tomatoes but you will need a very sharp knife and the above method is very quick.

With or without their skins, raw tomatoes can be flavoured with oregano, basil or fresh tarragon. Tomatoes can be cooked in the oven or frying pan. They can be stuffed with fresh mint, rice or bulgar wheat, pine nuts, minced meat and various cheeses (cream cheese, goat's cheese, ricotta or feta). Tomatoes become caramelised if they are roasted in the oven. Or they can be crushed and reduced to make a purée or coulis. They make excellent cream soups, baked custards and mousses.

You can use red tomatoes to make sorbets and desserts flavoured with dried fruit, while green tomatoes are good for sweet tarts and chutneys.

caramelised tomatoes

serves 4
preparation: 10 min
cooking: 1 hr 15 min

8 large tomatoes
5 tablespoons olive oil
salt and pepper

Preheat the oven to 230°C/450°F/Gas Mark 8.

Wash the tomatoes. Cut them in half and scoop out the seeds. Put them in an ovenproof dish, sprinkle them with olive oil and season, then put in the oven for 45 minutes. Reduce heat to 200°C/400°F/Gas Mark 6 and continue cooking for 30 min, then leave them to cool in the oven. (Check regularly during cooking as not all ovens are as accurate as they should be.)

Serve the caramelised tomatoes just as they are, sprinkled with fresh basil or with an accompaniment of cured ham.

tips

The tomato oil left over after cooking can be used to flavour another dish.

Caramelised tomatoes added to feta cheese and black olives, or to scrambled eggs, make a delicious filling for pitta bread.

Tomatoes colour and flavour olive oil during cooking. A few drops of this tomato-flavoured oil are enough to bring a taste of the sun to a green salad, simple spaghetti with basil, or a piece of ripe goat's cheese.

tartare of tomatoes with herbs

serves 6

preparation: 20 min

no cooking

10 firm tomatoes

1 shallot

1 bunch of basil

5 tablespoons olive oil

1 tablespoon balsamic vinegar

salt and pepper

Skin the tomatoes as described on page 50. Cut them in half to remove the seeds and squeeze them in your hand to remove the water. Peel the shallot. Rinse the bunch of basil, remove the leaves (discard the stalks) and dry them on kitchen paper. Chop all the ingredients separately.

Moisten the tomato pulp with olive oil and season with salt and pepper. Add the chopped shallot, basil and the balsamic vinegar. Mix everything together thoroughly. Arrange three little tomato tartares, shaped like mini-burgers, on each plate.

variations

Spread a light coating of oil over some thick slices of bread and cover with tomato tartare. This is reminiscent of the Spanish *pan y tomata* (bread rubbed with garlic and fresh tomato and sprinkled with olive oil).

As a change from the classic 'tomato mozzarella' you can replace the slices of tomato with the tartare.

tomatoes stuffed with goat's cheese and fresh thyme

serves 4
preparation: 15 min
cooking: 1 hr

8 firm tomatoes
250 g/9 oz goat's cheese
1 garlic clove
a few sprigs of fresh thyme
(or some dried thyme)
1 teaspoon olive oil
salt and pepper

Preheat the oven to 200°C/400°F/Gas Mark 6. Peel and finely chop the garlic and reserve.

Wash the tomatoes, cut a lid from the tops and put these to one side. Scoop out the insides and turn the tomatoes upside down to let the water drain.

Cut the goat's cheese into cubes and add salt and pepper. Divide the cheese into 8 and spoon into the tomatoes together with the thyme leaves and chopped garlic. Grease an ovenproof dish and place the tomatoes in it. Drizzle some olive oil over them and put the lids back on. Leave to cook in the oven for 1 hour.

tip
These tomatoes can also be cooked in the frying pan, over a high heat to begin with, then turned down to medium heat.

tomato and red pepper coulis

serves 4
preparation: 15 min
cooking: 40 min
refrigeration: 3 hr

1 kg/2¼ lb tomatoes
3 red peppers
2 garlic cloves
1 tablespoon olive oil
salt and pepper

Wash the tomatoes and peppers, then skin the tomatoes (see p. 50). Cut the tomatoes and peppers in half and remove the seeds. Peel and crush the garlic cloves. Heat the olive oil in a frying pan and sear the tomatoes and peppers. Add the crushed garlic, lower the heat and leave to simmer for 30 minutes. Remove from the heat and cool to room temperature.
Give the mixture a whizz in a food processor, or mash with a handheld blender or fork. Season with salt and pepper, then chill the coulis in the fridge for 3 hours.

mousse made with tomato and red pepper coulis

serves 4
preparation: 15 min
refrigeration: 12 hr

1 quantity of tomato and red pepper coulis (see above recipe)
1½ sachets powdered gelatine, or 5 gelatine leaves
150 ml/5 fl oz single cream
2 tablespoons mixed chopped tarragon and fresh basil
3 drops Tabasco®
2 tablespoons olive oil
salt and pepper

Heat up the tomato and red pepper coulis. Dissolve the powdered gelatine (or soften the gelatine leaves) as instructed on the packet and then add to the hot coulis. Beat vigorously with a whisk to make sure the gelatine is completely dissolved. Add the single cream, tarragon and basil mixture and Tabasco®. Mix well, adding salt and pepper if necessary. Grease a cake tin with olive oil and pour the mixture into it. Leave to set for 12 hours in the refrigerator, then serve well chilled.

penne rigate with tomato and red pepper coulis

serves 4
preparation: 5 min
cooking: 12 min
450 g/1lb penne rigate
1 quantity of tomato and red pepper coulis *(see recipe opposite)*
1 tablespoon olive oil
(or some black olives)
100 g/3½ oz freshly grated Parmesan
salt

Cook the penne as instructed on the packet until it is *al dente*. Reheat the coulis until it is very hot. Drain the pasta and pour the very hot tomato and red pepper coulis over it. Add a little olive oil (or finely chopped black olives) for flavour and serve sprinkled with Parmesan.

talking of eggs

soft- and hard-boiled eggs

no preparation
cooking: 5 min or 10 min

Put water on to boil in a small saucepan.
Lower the egg into it (the water must
cover it by at least ½ inch. (If there is
more than one egg, they should move
very little, so do not boil violently or they
could crack.)
Let the egg boil for 5 minutes if you just want
the yolk runny and 10 minutes if you want it
hard-boiled.

poached eggs

preparation: 5 min
cooking: 5 min

Pour an inch-depth of boiling water containing a little vinegar into a frying
pan placed over a gentle heat. Break each egg into a cup (without breaking
the yolk) and slide it into the water. Bring to the boil again, remove the
pan from the heat and cover with a lid. Leave for 3–4 minutes (when the egg
yolk should be covered by the set white), then carefully remove the egg
with a slotted spoon, let it drain (you can dab with kitchen paper) and
serve immediately.

scrambled eggs with caramelised tomatoes

serves 4
preparation: 3 min
cooking: 3 min

4 eggs

a little milk or single cream (optional)

knob of butter

8 caramelised tomatoes

(see recipe p. 51)

1 tablespoon chopped chives

salt and pepper

In a large bowl, whisk the eggs (with the milk or cream if using) and season. Melt the butter in a frying pan, then pour in the eggs and stir, using a wooden spoon. When the eggs have become firm and 'scrambled', remove the pan from the heat.

Divide the scrambled eggs between the plates and put 1 or 2 caramelised tomatoes on top of each serving. Season if necessary and sprinkle with chives, then dribble any tomato oil left from your caramelised tomatoes over the top.

eggs mimosa

serves 6
preparation: 10 min
cooking: 10 min

6 leaves from a Cos
or iceberg lettuce

6 hard-boiled eggs

4 tablespoons mayonnaise

2 lemons

salt and pepper

Wash and dry the lettuce leaves and put to one side.

Remove the shells from the eggs and cut them in half lengthways. Carefully remove the yolks and mash them with a fork. In a bowl, mix half the mashed egg yolks with the mayonnaise and season to taste, then use the mixture to fill the egg halves.

Arrange the lettuce leaves on a large plate or serving dish, and put two filled egg halves on each. Scatter the remaining egg yolks over the top.

Serve this dish accompanied by the lemons cut into quarters.

spanish tortilla

serves 6
preparation: 10 min
cooking: 40 min

5 potatoes
1 onion
6 tablespoons olive oil
8 eggs
a few sprigs of fresh thyme
salt and pepper

Peel the potatoes, cut them into cubes, and rinse off the starch. Peel and chop the onion. Heat the olive oil in a frying pan and put in the potatoes and onion to cook for about 30 minutes over a medium heat, stirring often.

Whisk the eggs with salt and pepper in a large bowl and pour over the potatoes, lower the heat and leave to cook gently until the underside is firm. Slide the omelette on to a plate, return it uncooked side onto the frying pan and cover. When this underside is also firm, take your tortilla off the heat and serve straight away, garnished with sprigs of fresh thyme, and accompanied by a green salad or tomatoes.

omelette with crisps

serves 4
preparation: 10 min
cooking: 3 min

6 eggs
2 tablespoons olive oil
3 handfuls of crisps, plain or
flavoured, according to taste
salt and pepper

Whisk the eggs in a large bowl, adding seasoning carefully as the crisps will be salty. Heat the olive oil in a frying pan, pour in the eggs and let them cook over a medium heat, tipping the pan from side to side occasionally.

Crush the crisps in your hands and sprinkle over the eggs, which should still be moist. With the aid of a spatula, fold one half of the omelette over on to the other.

Serve immediately while the crisps remain crunchy.

caesar salad

serves 4
preparation: 15 min
cooking: 2 min

for the salad
1 Cos lettuce
100 g/3½ oz piece of Parmesan
7 thick slices fresh bread or sandwich
loaf (or the equivalent of ready-to-
use croutons)
1 tablespoon olive oil
4 hard-boiled eggs, for garnish

for the dressing
1 garlic clove
5 anchovy fillets (or 1 tablespoon
anchovy paste)
1 teaspoon strong mustard
juice of ½ lemon
4 tablespoons olive oil
pepper

Make sure you don't add any salt; the anchovies are already salty enough.

To make your Caesar salad into a special dish, just add some sliced, cooked chicken breast.

To prepare the salad: Wash and dry the lettuce leaves, tearing the larger leaves into pieces. Cut shavings of Parmesan using a vegetable peeler or a knife with a sharp blade. Remove the crusts from the slices of bread and cut the bread into dice. Heat the oil in a frying pan and fry the diced bread until brown and crunchy. Remove the croutons from the pan and leave to drain on kitchen paper to remove any excess oil.

To prepare the dressing: Peel and chop the garlic, and mash the anchovy fillets (if using) with a fork. Place the garlic and anchovies in a bowl and mix in the mustard and lemon juice. Add some pepper and mix again. Now add the olive oil little by little, stirring all the time, until the sauce begins to thicken.

In a large salad bowl, toss together the sauce, lettuce, Parmesan and croutons. Add more pepper if necessary.

Arrange the salad on the plates and garnish with the hard-boiled eggs cut into quarters.

salade niçoise

serves 4
preparation: 20 min
cooking: 10 min

for the salad
200 g/7 oz tin tuna
8 anchovy fillets in olive oil
3 hard-boiled eggs
1 onion (preferably red)
4 plum or vine tomatoes
3 sticks celery
200 g/7 oz green beans, fresh or
frozen
100 g/3½ oz stoned black olives
(preferably Nice olives)
2 tablespoons freshly chopped basil
2 tablespoons capers

for the dressing
1 garlic clove
4 tablespoons olive oil
juice of 1 lemon
salt and pepper

To prepare the salad: Drain the tuna and anchovies. Shell the eggs and cut them into quarters. Peel and slice the onion into rings. Wash and cut the tomatoes in half, scoop out the pips and slice each half into three. Cut the celery into thin strips, top and tail the green beans and cook both vegetables for about 10 minutes in a saucepan of boiling water (if using frozen beans follow the packet instructions). Drain, refresh in cold water and drain again.

To prepare the dressing: Peel and chop the garlic clove and mix with the olive oil, lemon juice and seasoning in a bowl.

To serve, divide the vegetables, eggs, anchovies and crumbled tuna between the plates. Garnish with the black olives, basil and capers, and pour the dressing over the top.

coleslaw

serves 4
preparation: 15 min
no cooking

for the salad
½ white cabbage
1 eating apple
250 g/9 oz carrots, grated
1 tablespoon chopped parsley
2 tablespoons capers
2 tablespoons chopped gherkins

for the dressing
3 tablespoons mayonnaise
1 teaspoon seasoned French
mustard
1 teaspoon paprika
2 tablespoons olive oil
juice of 1 lemon
salt and pepper

To prepare the salad: Wash and finely shred the cabbage. Wash the apple, core and cut into cubes. Place the cabbage and apple in a salad bowl, add the carrot, parsley, capers and gherkins.

To prepare the dressing: Put all the ingredients into a bowl and briskly whisk together. Pour into the salad bowl and toss thoroughly.

Serve the coleslaw on its own or with meat, poultry, fish or jacket potatoes.

monsieur henri's steak tartare

serves 4

preparation: 10 min + 1 hr

resting time

no cooking

3 egg yolks

2 tablespoons strong mustard

2 tablespoons Worcestershire sauce®

juice of ½ lemon

few drops Tabasco®

3 tablespoons olive oil

2 tablespoons chopped gherkins

2 tablespoons chopped capers

2 tablespoons chopped fresh parsley

2 tablespoons chopped fresh chives

600 g/1 lb 5 oz lean steak mince

salt and pepper

In a large bowl, mix together the egg yolks, mustard, Worcestershire sauce®, lemon juice, Tabasco® and salt. Beat the sauce until it thickens like a mayonnaise, mixing vigorously with a whisk or a fork while gradually adding the oil. Add some more salt if necessary, together with some pepper. Gently fold in the gherkins and capers, then the parsley and chives.

Pour the mixture over the meat and combine it all thoroughly, using your hands. Allow to rest in the fridge for an hour or so to let the flavours mingle. Shape into 4 mounds, or patties, with your hands and arrange on the plates.

tips

To prevent the meat turning into a pâté when you add the seasoning, make sure it is minced coarsely.

If you don't want to kill the meat flavour, go easy on the Tabasco®.

Dear Mum,

Have you tried the Italian version of steak tartare? You make it with 1 egg yolk, chives, Tabasco®, 50 g/2 oz Parmesan shavings, 50 g freshly chopped basil, 2 tablespoons chopped capers, mustard, 1 tablespoon balsamic vinegar, 2 tablespoons olive oil, salt and pepper. It's not bad at all!

beef and bacon hamburger

serves 4
preparation: 15 min
cooking: 15 min

1 tablespoon olive oil
4 bacon rashers
500 g/1 lb 2 oz minced beef
1 Cos or iceberg lettuce
1 large tomato
1 onion
4 hamburger buns with sesame
seeds

for the hamburger sauce
2 teaspoons seasoned mustard
1 tablespoon Worcestershire sauce®
1 tablespoon chopped chives
4 drops Tabasco®
1 tablespoon olive oil
salt and pepper

To prepare the hamburger sauce: Mix together all the ingredients.

Heat the oil in a frying pan and cook the bacon rashers. Remove them from the pan and keep warm. Form the minced beef into 4 burgers. Reheat the frying pan and sear the burgers on both sides, then leave to cook according to how well done you like your burgers.

Wash and dry 4 lettuce leaves; wash the tomato and cut into 4 slices. Peel the onion and slice it into 4 as well. Cut the buns in half, and put a lettuce leaf, a rasher of bacon and a burger on the bottom halves. Cover this with the hamburger sauce and a slice of tomato followed by a slice of onion. Put the other half of the bun back on top.

Serve accompanied by tomato ketchup® or another favourite hamburger sauce.

variations

With the same hamburger sauce and keeping the bacon, replace the minced beef with prawns or chicken breast, either just as it is or fried in breadcrumbs.

For a vegetarian hamburger, use avocado slices, hard-boiled eggs and sweetcorn in place of the bacon and meat.

beef à la mode

serves 4
preparation: 10 min
cooking: 4 hr

1 kg/2¼ lb shin or stewing beef
2 onions
1 garlic clove
2 tablespoons olive oil
200 g/7 oz streaky bacon, diced
2 glasses red wine
400 ml/14 fl oz water
1 kg/2¼ lb carrots
2 sprigs of thyme
1 bay leaf
1 clove (optional)
salt and pepper

Cut the meat into 3-cm cubes.
Peel and cut the onions and garlic clove in half. Heat the oil in a flameproof casserole dish and put in the onion and garlic. Give them a stir and add the diced bacon. Brown them all together and then transfer to a plate. In the casserole, brown the meat cubes on all sides. Then pour in the wine and water and let it reduce over a medium heat. Meanwhile, peel of and slice the carrots. Put the reserved onion, garlic and bacon back in, and mix together.
Add the carrots to the casserole together with the thyme, bay leaf and clove (optional). Leave to simmer over very low heat for 3–4 hours, stirring occasionally. Do not let the meat overcook, or you will have lovely gravy but tasteless meat.

tip
For added flavour, cook your beef à la mode the day before. It's better reheated.

If you have some beef à la mode left over, you can serve it cold the following day, as a salad, with some gherkins.

ratatouille

serves 4
preparation: 20 min
cooking: 35 min

2 courgettes
1 large aubergine
2 red or green peppers
400 g/14 oz fresh or tinned plum
tomatoes (well-drained)
1 onion
2 garlic cloves
4 tablespoons olive oil
1 tablespoon tomato purée
1 tablespoon paprika
1 tablespoon dried Mediterranean
herbs
salt and pepper

Wash the vegetables, remove the seeds from the peppers and cut into 1-cm strips. Cut the tomatoes into quarters, the courgettes into thick slices and the aubergines into 2-cm cubes. Peel and chop the onion and garlic. Heat a tablespoon of olive oil in a pan. After 3 minutes add the tomatoes , onion and garlic, and cook for 5 minutes, stirring from time to time. Remove the tomato mixture from the pan and set aside in a dish. In the same pan, soften all the other vegetables separately for 2–3 minutes, using 1 tablespoon of olive oil each time.

Put all the sautéed vegetables back into the pan together and add the garlic, onion and tomato mixture, 1 tablespoon of tomato purée, the paprika, then the Mediterranean herbs, salt and pepper. Leave to simmer, covered, over a low heat for 35 minutes, stirring occasionally. The vegetables should be soft but retain their individuality – do not let them become mushy.

Serve with fried eggs, meat or rice.

spaghetti bolognaise

serves 4
preparation: 15 min
cooking: 40 min
450 g/1 lb spaghetti
100 g/3½ oz freshly grated Parmesan
salt

for the bolognaise sauce
1 onion
1 garlic clove
2 tablespoons olive oil
500 g/1 lb 2 oz minced beef
400 g/14 oz tin peeled tomatoes
1 small tin tomato purée
salt and pepper

To prepare the bolognaise sauce: Peel and finely chop the onion and garlic, then heat the oil in a saucepan and soften them. Then add the mince, season with salt and pepper, mix together and brown over a medium heat. Stir in the tomatoes and tomato purée. Cover and leave to simmer gently for 40 minutes. Bring a large pan of salted water to the boil, add the spaghetti and follow the cooking time indicated on the packet so that it is *al dente* when ready. Drain the pasta.
Serve the spaghetti covered with the sauce, with a bowl of grated Parmesan on the side.

penne carbonara

serves 4
preparation: 15 min
cooking: 15 min
450 g/1 lb penne rigate
1 tablespoon olive oil
200 g/7 oz streaky bacon, diced
200 ml/7 fl oz crème fraîche
3 egg yolks
100 g/3½ oz freshly grated Parmesan
salt

Cook the penne in boiling salted water to the packet instructions until *al dente*. Meanwhile, heat the olive oil in a frying pan and brown the diced bacon. Pour half the crème fraîche over them, stir and switch off the heat. Stir in the remaining crème fraîche and the egg yolks, diluting the mixture with a little of the cooking water from the pasta. Drain the penne pour the sauce over the top, stir to coat the penne and sprinkle with Parmesan.

You can replace fresh mushrooms with frozen ones. And there's no reason why you shouldn't use asparagus instead, either fresh, tinned or frozen.

serves 4

preparation: 15 min

cooking: 40 min

1 onion

1 garlic clove

350 g/12 oz mixed mushrooms

4 courgettes

80 g/3 oz butter

2 tablespoons chopped flat-leaf parsley

1 glass of white wine

300 g/10 oz risotto rice (arborio)

1½ litres/2¾ pints chicken stock

1 tablespoon olive oil

70 g/2½ oz grated Parmesan (+ a few shavings)

few rocket leaves

salt and pepper

mushroom risotto

Peel and finely chop the onion and garlic. Wipe the mushrooms with a damp cloth, peel if necessary, and chop coarsely. Peel the courgettes and cut into chunks.

Melt the butter in a large saucepan, add the onion and garlic and soften for 5 minutes. Mix in the mushrooms, courgettes and parsley, together with some seasoning, and cook over a medium heat for 3 minutes. Pour in the wine and let it cook until the liquid has completely evaporated. Add the rice and mix well to coat the grains. To be creamy and remain slightly firm, the rice has to absorb the stock very gradually so add it, half a cupful at a time, allowing each addition to be absorbed before adding the next.

Check the seasoning; sprinkle over 1 tablespoon of olive oil (or add a knob of butter) and a little of the grated Parmesan. Stir thoroughly to ensure the ingredients are well mixed.

Serve immediately, garnished with rocket leaves and shavings of Parmesan, with a bowl of Parmesan on the side.

fish and chips, french-style

serves 4

preparation: 10 min

cooking: 35 min

675 g/1½ lb potatoes

oil for frying

30 g/1 oz plain flour

250 g/9 oz dried breadcrumbs

2 tablespoons milk

3 egg whites

8 large (or 12 small) white fish fillets (cod, whiting, etc.)

salt

Dear Mum,

You can buy oven-ready chips from the freezer cabinets in food shops. But best of all, for fish and 'chips', are crisps (plain, cheese, barbecue flavour or salt and vinegar ...).

Peel the potatoes, cut them in half lengthways, rinse off the starch, dry on kitchen paper and then cut into chips. Put 4 tablespoons of oil in a frying pan to get very hot and then add the potatoes to brown over a very high heat. Continue cooking for about 30 minutes over a moderate heat, adding more oil if necessary. Spread out the flour and breadcrumbs on two separate plates and, in a large bowl, mix the milk and egg whites.

Coat the fish fillets in flour, then in egg white and finally in breadcrumbs. Cook for 20 minutes, either in a preheated oven (220°C/425°F/ Gas Mark 7) on a greased baking sheet, or in a deep frying pan in 4 tablespoons of oil.

Add salt to the fish and chips, before serving them accompanied by a yogurt and herb sauce.

talking of potatoes

Waxy potatoes are best for boiling (in their skins), sautéing or frying. For mashed potato and gratins, it's better to buy floury potatoes. Supermarket packaging indicates which variety is suitable for which use.

quantities

It's usual to allow more or less 1 kg/2 $\frac{1}{4}$ lb of potatoes for 4 people.

the various cooking methods

In their skins (boiled): scrub, then plunge them skin and all into a large saucepan of cold salted water. After they've cooked for about 30 minutes (depending on their size), they can be eaten hot, accompanied by cream cheese with fine herbs or simply with salt and butter.

When they are cold, you can peel them and cut into thick slices for canapés. And, diced or sliced, they make excellent salads when put together with herring, tuna, chicken, olives, celery and so on.

Fried in oil or butter: in slices, cubes, peeled or unpeeled … raw potatoes need about 40 minutes' cooking time. Parboiled before frying, they cook more quickly – you need to reckon on about 10 minutes.

In foil: whole raw potatoes with their scrubbed skins left on and pricked with a fork take about 1 hour to cook in a hot oven (230°C/450°F/Gas Mark 8). Wrap each one separately in foil.

Boulangère: peeled or unpeeled, potatoes can roast in the same dish at the same time as a piece of red meat or chicken.

mashed potatoes

serves 4
preparation: 5 min
cooking: 30 min

1 kg/2¼ lb potatoes
200 ml/7 fl oz milk
600 ml/1 pint water
1 garlic clove
1 bay leaf
1 teaspoon ground nutmeg
50 g/2 oz butter
200 ml/7 fl oz single cream
salt and pepper

Wash and peel the potatoes. Cut them into quarters. Put them in a saucepan with the milk, water, peeled garlic clove, bay leaf, nutmeg, salt and pepper. Let them cook over a medium heat for 30 minutes (until they start to collapse). Drain and discard the bay leaf. Mash the potatoes with a fork while you add the butter and cream. A bowl of mashed potato will keep hot if placed over a saucepan containing simmering water.

gratin dauphinois

serves 4
preparation: 10 min
cooking: 50 min

200 ml/7 fl oz milk
200 ml/7 fl oz single cream
1 kg/2¼ lb potatoes
25 g/1 oz butter
salt and pepper

Preheat the oven to 220°C/425°F/Gas Mark 7. In a bowl, combine the milk, single cream, salt and pepper. Peel the potatoes and cut them into thin slices. Grease a gratin dish with the butter, arrange the potato slices and cover them with the milk and cream mixture. Bake in the oven for about 50 minutes.

rice pudding

serves 4
preparation: 5 min
cooking: 15 min

1 litre/1¾ pints milk
150 g/5 oz caster sugar
1 vanilla pod or 1 teaspoon vanilla extract
250 g/9 oz round-grain pudding rice
brown sugar or cinnamon

Put the milk, sugar and vanilla pod, slit in two, into a saucepan. When the milk is just simmering (it must not boil), turn down the heat. Remove the vanilla pod, scrape out the seeds and put them back into the milk. Add the rice and stir continuously over a gentle heat it has absorbed all the liquid.

Serve warm or cold, in a large bowl or in individual ones, sprinkled with brown sugar or cinnamon.

pain perdu

serves 4
preparation: 5 min
cooking: 5 min

2 eggs
200 ml/7 fl oz milk
3 tablespoons caster sugar
50 g/2 oz butter
8 good slices of bread (preferably stale)

Break the eggs into a large bowl and whisk them vigorously while adding the milk and sugar. Melt the butter in the frying pan, dip the slices of bread in the egg mixture and fry them on both sides until they are a nice golden brown. Serve immediately.

nutella® creams

serves 4
preparation: 20 min
no cooking
refrigeration: 8 hr

for the cream
175 g/6 oz Nutella®
300 ml/10 fl oz whipping cream
(keep a little aside for serving)

for the truffles
10 spicy biscuits (ginger snaps or
another favourite)
250 g/9 oz Nutella®
150 ml/5 oz crème fraîche

To prepare the cream: Beat the Nutella® and cream together with a whisk. Pour the mixture into 4 cups and leave in the fridge for 8 hours.
To prepare the truffles: Crush the biscuits and put them in a dish. Mix the Nutella® with the crème fraîche and one third of the biscuit crumbs. Put in the fridge to chill. After 20 minutes, remove the mixture from the fridge and shape into about 20 small balls by rolling them lightly between the palms of your hands. Roll each ball in the remaining crumbs.
To serve, put a truffle in a teaspoon on each plate, together with a cup of the Nutella® cream topped by a little whipped cream. Serve the remaining truffles separately as an accompaniment.

dark chocolate truffles

makes about 20 truffles
preparation: 15 min
no cooking
refrigeration: 4 hr
250 g/9 oz dark chocolate
50 g/2 oz butter
150 ml/5 oz crème fraîche
cocoa powder

Melt the chocolate, butter and crème fraîche over a very low heat, stirring all the time, then place the mixture in the refrigerator for 4 hours.
Make about 20 little balls by rolling them lightly between the palms of your hands. Then roll in the cocoa powder.

cheesecake

serves 8–10
preparation: 15 min
cooking: 1 hr

100 g/3½ oz shortbread biscuits
125 g/4½ oz ground almonds
50 g/2 oz butter, melted
600 g/1 lb 5 oz fromage frais,
or cream cheese
225 g/8 oz caster sugar
200 ml/7 oz thick crème fraîche
4 eggs
1 tablespoon grated lemon rind

Butter a cake tin with a loose base and cover the base with crushed shortbread biscuits mixed with the ground almonds and melted butter. Put in the refrigerator, then preheat the oven to 180°C/350°F/Gas Mark 4.
Drain the fromage frais and put it in a bowl with the sugar and crème fraîche. Add the eggs and lemon rind and whisk the mixture until it is light and fluffy. Pour it over the biscuit base and bake for about 1 hour. Allow to cool before chilling in the fridge. Serve with fruit, a coulis, or lemon curd.

pancakes

makes 12 pancakes
preparation: 10 min
standing time: 1 hr
cooking: 5 min for each pancake

250 g/9 oz plain flour
2 teaspoons baking powder
400 ml/14 fl oz milk
100 ml/3½ fl oz single cream
30 g/1 oz butter, melted
caster sugar
1 whole egg and 2 whites
knob of butter
salt

Sift the flour, baking powder and salt into a large bowl. In another bowl whisk together the milk, cream, melted butter, sugar, whole egg and 2 egg whites. Make a well in the flour and incorporate the liquid mixture, beating to remove lumps. Leave to stand for 1 hour.
Heat a small frying pan and grease it with a piece of buttery absorbent kitchen paper. Pour in a small ladleful of batter. When bubbles appear on the surface, turn the pancake over. Let it cook until it is nice and golden. Cook the rest of the pancakes in the same way. Serve with caster sugar.

rediscover your favourite dishes

hummus

serves 4

preparation: 10 min

no cooking

300 g/10 oz tinned chickpeas

1 garlic clove

3 tablespoons sesame seed paste
(tahina)

juice of 2–3 lemons

2 tablespoons freshly chopped
coriander

6 tablespoons olive oil

1 teaspoon ground paprika

salt and pepper

Rinse and drain the chickpeas. Peel the garlic clove and cut it in half. Put the chickpeas, sesame paste, juice of 2 lemons, garlic, 1 tablespoon of the coriander, 5 tablespoons of the olive oil, salt and pepper into the bowl of your food processor or liquidiser, and mix until you obtain a smooth paste. Add more lemon juice or a little water if it is too thick.

Transfer to a shallow bowl and place in the refrigerator. Before serving, sprinkle with paprika and the remaining coriander, and drizzle over the remaining olive oil.

You can also mash chickpeas with a fork.

roasted peppers

serves 4
preparation: 10 min
cooking: 30 min
4 large red or green peppers

Preheat the oven to 230°C/450°F/Gas Mark 8. Wash the peppers and put them in an oiled ovenproof dish. Roast for 30 minutes until their skins start to wrinkle. Remove from the oven to cool a little, then peel them and scoop out the seeds.

roasted peppers marinated in garlic

serves 4
preparation: 20 min
cooking: 30 min
refrigeration: 20 min
4 large red or green peppers
$\frac{1}{2}$ garlic clove, chopped
olive oil
salt and pepper

Prepare the roasted peppers from the recipe above, then cut into strips and arrange them in a dish with the garlic. Season and sprinkle with olive oil. Place in the refrigerator 20 minutes before serving.

tip
You can liven up the marinade by adding rosemary, thyme or a bay leaf.

85

stuffed peppers

serves 4
preparation: 20 min
cooking: 30 min

8 small peppers
2 teaspoons of chopped mixed
herbs (chives, thyme, parsley …),
or fresh mint
350 g/12 oz ricotta
olive oil

In place of ricotta you can sometimes find tins of brandade of salt cod in a good deli. To tone down its strong flavour, you can mix in a little milk or single cream, but don't add any salt as it's already salted. Just add some pepper.

Roast the peppers in the oven *(see recipe p. 85)*, then peel and deseed them. Add the chopped mixed herbs or fresh mint to the ricotta and fill the peppers. Serve sprinkled with a little olive oil.

chouchouka (tunisian speciality)

serves 4
preparation: 15 min
cooking: 45 min

4 red or green peppers
6 very ripe tomatoes
2 garlic cloves
olive oil
salt and pepper

Cut the peppers into strips. Skin *(see p. 50)* and deseed the tomatoes, then crush the garlic cloves. In an oiled frying pan or saucepan, cook the tomatoes and garlic over a medium heat. Halfway through the cooking time, add the strips of pepper and season with salt and pepper.

ricotta with mixed herbs

makes I large bowl
preparation: 5 min
no cooking
250 g/9 oz tub ricotta
4 tablespoons chopped chives
4 tablespoons chopped parsley
4 tablespoons chopped basil
olive oil
salt and pepper

Crumble the ricotta and mix it in a large bowl with the chives, parsley and basil. Add some olive oil and season.

variation
You can replace the ricotta with soft goat's milk cheese, and add thyme, rosemary and finely chopped black olives.

tzatziki

serves 4
preparation: 5 min
no cooking
refrigeration: 4 hr
2 cucumbers
I garlic clove
8 sprigs of chives
10 fresh mint leaves
500 g/18 oz Greek yogurt
I tablespoon olive oil
juice from $\frac{1}{2}$ lemon
salt and pepper

Peel the cucumbers, remove the seeds and cut the flesh into small cubes. Peel and chop the garlic, finely snip the chives with scissors and chop the mint leaves. Tip the yogurt into a serving bowl, add all the other ingredients and mix well together. Serve well chilled.

aubergine slices
with tomato, parmesan and basil

serves 4
preparation: 10 min
cooking: 4 min

2 aubergines
olive oil
1 small tin tomato purée
1 bunch fresh basil, chopped
freshly grated Parmesan

Preheat the oven to 230°C/450°F/Gas Mark 8. Wash the aubergines and slice them thinly lengthways. Dab them lightly with oil on each side before laying them on a baking tray covered with greaseproof paper. Let them cook for about 3 minutes, then remove from the oven.

Before serving, heat the grill and spread a thin layer of tomato purée over the aubergine slices. Sprinkle them with basil and Parmesan and then with olive oil, and place under the grill for 1 minute. Serve the slices rolled up and secured with a wooden cocktail stick.

aubergine caviar

for 1 large bowl
preparation: 5 min
cooking: 45 min
refrigeration: 8 hr

2 aubergines
2 teaspoons onion powder
2 teaspoons garlic powder
2 teaspoons tomato purée
3 tablespoons olive oil
juice of 1 lemon
salt and pepper

Preheat the oven to 220°C/425°F/Gas Mark 7.

Wash the aubergines and put them in the oven until their skins begin to blacken and split. Peel them when they are cool enough to handle.

Mash the pulp and sprinkle it with the onion and garlic powders. Add the tomato purée, the olive oil and lemon juice. Season and mix together well. Leave it in the fridge for at least 8 hours before serving.

chicken liver pâté

serves 4
preparation: 15 min
cooking: 15 min
refrigeration: 8 hr

250 g/9 oz chicken livers
olive oil
2 shallots
1 large garlic clove
1 tablespoon chopped fresh parsley
2 teaspoons crushed coriander seeds
1 hard-boiled egg
1 teaspoon vinegar
salt and pepper

You can replace the hard-boiled egg with crumbled rusk.

Wash the chicken livers and dry them on kitchen paper. Then fry them in olive oil over a moderate heat for about 5 minutes. They should be just cooked through and certainly not rubbery! Remove from the pan and leave on kitchen paper.

Peel and chop the shallots and garlic and soften in the olive oil. When they begin to brown, add the parsley and coriander seeds. Add the hard-boiled egg, chopped into small pieces, together with the vinegar, salt and pepper. Add the chicken livers and mix all the ingredients, crushing them with a fork. Transfer the mixture to a large bowl or cake tin, tamping it down well, and leave in the fridge for 8 hours before serving.

variation

For a liver mousse, whizz all the ingredients in a food processor instead of mashing them with a fork.

tomato and italian ham bruschetta

serves 4
preparation: 5 min
cooking: 2 min
4 slices bread
2 tomatoes
1 garlic clove
4 thin slices Italian ham (Parma,
San Daniele, etc.)
olive oil

Toast the bread and wash the tomatoes. Peel the garlic clove and rub the toasted slices of bread with garlic and cover with sliced tomato. Scatter strips of ham over them and sprinkle with olive oil.

variation
Instead of ham, you can use anchovies, shavings of Parmesan, or fresh goat's cheese.

cannellini bean salad with thyme and basil

serves 4
preparation: 10 min
cooking: 30 min
2–3 ripe tomatos
1 onion
2 garlic cloves
3 tablespoons olive oil
1 teaspoon fresh (or dried) thyme
leaves
200 g/7 oz tinned cannellini beans
4 tablespoons chopped fresh basil
salt and pepper

Skin the tomatoes *(see p. 50)* and peel and thickly slice the onion. Peel and crush the garlic cloves. Heat 2 tablespoons of the olive oil in a saucepan and soften the onion and garlic, add the tomatoes, crushing them with a fork, and the thyme. Simmer gently for 10–15 minutes. Rinse and drain the beans and add to the sauce to warm through. Transfer to a serving bowl, add the remaining tablespoon of olive oil and the basil.
Mix and serve warm.

carrot and almond salad

serves 6
preparation: 15 min
cooking: 1 min

10 fresh carrots, 1 cucumber
100 g/3½ oz raisins
100 g/3½ oz flaked almonds
1 tablespoon honey
1 teaspoon ground ginger
1 teaspoon ground cinnamon
3 tablespoons olive oil
juice of ½ a lemon
salt and pepper

For the salad: Peel and grate the carrots. Peel the cucumber and cut it in half lengthways, remove the seeds and cut the flesh into cubes. In a large salad bowl, mix the carrots, cucumber and raisins. Toast the flaked almonds in a frying pan for a minute, stirring to stop them burning.

For the dressing: In a bowl, mix the honey, ginger, cinnamon, 3 tablespoons olive oil, lemon juice, and salt and pepper. Then add to the salad and toss well.

Garnish with the toasted almonds. Serve chilled.

carrot and green olive salad

serves 6
preparation: 10 min
cooking: 25 min
refrigeration: 2 hr

10 fresh carrots
1 garlic clove
250 g/9 oz stoned green olives
1 teaspoon ground cumin
1 teaspoon ground cinnamon
juice of 1 lemon
3 tablespoons olive oil
salt and pepper
fresh coriander, to garnish

Peel the carrots and slice into rounds. Boil them in a saucepan of lightly salted water until they are cooked through but still holding their shape. Drain and set aside.

Peel and chop the garlic clove, then soften it in a lightly oiled frying pan, and add the carrots and olives. Cook for 2 minutes.

In a salad bowl, mix the cumin, cinnamon, lemon juice and olive oil, and add the carrots and olives. Season to taste and mix again. Serve the salad chilled, garnished with chopped coriander.

couscous with dates and walnuts

serves 6
preparation: 10 min
cooking: 10 min
$\frac{1}{2}$ vegetable stock cube
400 g/14 oz couscous
butter
olive oil
200 g/7 oz dates
200 g/7 oz green walnuts
200 g/7 oz tinned chickpeas
ground cinnamon

Put the half stock cube into 1 litre of boiling water. Remove from the heat, pour in the couscous and leave it to swell for 3–4 minutes. Add a knob of butter and stir. If the grains of couscous are not cooked through, put it back over a very low heat.

Flavour the couscous with a few drops of olive oil, then fluff it up with a fork so that it becomes light and the grains separate from one another. Roughly chop the dates and green walnuts and add to the couscous followed by the rinsed and drained chickpeas.

Put the couscous in a shallow bowl or serving dish so that it forms a dome, and sprinkle with cinnamon.

variation

Couscous can be combined with many other things. With chickpeas as the basic ingredient, you can add strips of grilled pepper, raisins and pine kernels, or strips of roasted pepper with roasted onion, cubes of carrot and courgette, or sliced carrots with diced turnips and courgettes.

As regards herbs, coriander leaves or fresh chives go well with couscous. And good spices to use are cinnamon, cumin, ginger and paprika, which all add a nice flavour.

Dear Mum,
Couscous can be cooked in a frying pan too – what I do is heat some olive oil and put it into the hot pan. Then I toast the grains slightly because I like the taste, and add some water flavoured with a vegetable stock cube. I mix it all up and then leave it to swell away from the heat. If the grains aren't cooked enough, I put it back over a low heat and add a drop of water. Then I fluff it up with a fork.

Dear Mum,
A friend came round to work at my place and decided to stay for lunch. I mixed up some leftovers from kefta tagine, mashing it all together. Then I added some feta cheese and black olives, lemon juice and a tiny bit of olive oil, and used it as a baguette filling. Yummy!!!

kefta tagine

serves 6
preparation: 20 min
cooking: 50 min

for the tomato sauce
1 onion
2 garlic cloves
1 tablespoon olive oil
1 tablespoon ground cumin
1 tablespoon paprika
2 x 400 g/14 oz tins peeled,
chopped tomatoes
salt and pepper

for the keftas
1 onion
1 bunch of fresh mint
1 bunch of flat-leaf parsley
800 g/1¾ lb minced beef
2 eggs
1 tablespoon ground cumin
1 tablespoon paprika
1 teaspoon cinnamon
2 tablespoons olive oil
salt and pepper

To prepare the tomato sauce: Peel and chop the onion. Peel the garlic cloves and crush with the flat of a knife blade. Heat the olive oil in a frying pan and put the garlic and onion in to soften. Add the spices and tomatoes. Season and leave to simmer over a low heat while you are making the keftas.

To prepare the keftas: Peel and chop the onion. Wash, dry and chop the mint and flat-leaf parsley. In a large bowl, combine the onion, half the mint and parsley, the raw meat, eggs, spices, salt and pepper. Shape this mixture into little balls by taking pieces of the mixture and rolling it between the palms of your hands. Heat the olive oil in a frying pan, brown the meat balls and add them to the tomato sauce. Leave to simmer gently for about 30 minutes. Serve sprinkled with the remaining chopped mint and parsley.

tip
This is an ideal recipe for the tagine pot, baked in the oven at 200°C/400°F/Gas Mark 6.

chicken tagine with olives

serves 6
preparation: 10 min
cooking: 1 hr 30 min

2 onions

3 garlic cloves

juice and rind of 3 lemons

1 tablespoon ground cumin

1 tablespoon ground paprika

1 teaspoon ground ginger

1 teaspoon ground cinnamon

5 tablespoons olive oil

juice of 1 orange

1 bunch fresh coriander, chopped

200 ml/7 fl oz water

12 chicken pieces

(with or without skin)

1 preserved lemon

250 g/9 oz stoned green (or black)

olives

salt and pepper

Peel and chop the onions and garlic. Squeeze the lemons and reserve the juice; scrub the rind and pare the zest into fine strips. Put the zest strips in a bowl with the spices, 3 table-spoons of olive oil, the orange and lemon juice, half the bunch of chopped fresh corian-der, salt, pepper and the water. Mix well and put to one side.

Brown the chicken pieces in a frying pan for a few minutes with 1 tablespoon of olive oil. Spread a tablespoon of olive oil over the bot-tom of a tagine dish or casserole and arrange the browned chicken pieces in it. Sprinkle over the chopped onions and garlic, pieces of preserved lemon and the olives. Now pour the contents of the bowl over it. Cover and leave to cook over low heat or in the oven at 180°C/350°F/Gas Mark 4 for at least $1\frac{1}{2}$ hours. Check regularly and top up with water if necessary.

Serve garnished with the remaining corian-der.

tip

To check for doneness, the chicken juices must run clear when pierced deeply with a sharp skewer.

orange salad with saffron and olive oil

serves 6
preparation: 15 min
cooking: 3 min
refrigeration: 20 min

10 oranges
50 g/2 oz caster sugar
1 teaspoon honey
pinch of saffron threads
3 tablespoons olive oil

Squeeze 2 oranges and pour the juice into a saucepan. Add the sugar and honey and dissolve over a low heat. Leave to cool to room temperature.

Peel the other oranges, removing the white pith, and cut them into slices. Arrange them on a large plate (preferably a transparent or ceramic one) and pour over the cooled orange syrup. Sprinkle some saffron over the top and then some olive oil. Serve chilled.

poached pears with saffron and vanilla syrup

serves 4
preparation: 5 min
cooking: 30 min

4 pears
1 vanilla pod or 1 teaspoon vanilla extract
500 ml/18 fl oz water
200 g/7 oz sugar
1 tablespoon ground ginger
pinch of saffron threads
1 lemon, scrubbed
4 juicy, stoned dates

Peel the pears, keeping them whole.

Cut the vanilla pod in half and scoop out the seeds, then put the cut pod, together with the seeds, into a saucepan with the water, sugar, ginger, saffron, and pared zest from the lemon. Bring to the boil while stirring.

Remove from the heat and put the pears into the boiling syrup, return the saucepan to the hob, lower the heat and let the pears poach for about 20 minutes. They should be cooked through but still firm (check with a sharp skewer). Serve, hot or chilled, in a large bowl or in individual glass bowls, with some of the syrup and decorated with halved dates.

apples bonne femme

serves 4
preparation: 10 min
cooking: 20 min

1 tablespoon raisins

150 ml/5 fl oz apple juice

rind and juice of $\frac{1}{2}$ lemon

4 cooking apples

2 tablespoons flaked almonds

1 tablespoon honey

$\frac{1}{2}$ teaspoon ground cinnamon

knob of butter

Put the raisins in the apple juice to swell up, and then preheat the oven to 200°C/400°F/ Gas Mark 6.

Pare the rind from the half lemon, wash it and cut into very thin strips and then into tiny pieces. Squeeze 2 tablespoons of juice from the half lemon; put the rind and the juice to one side.

Wash and dry the apples and cut a lid from the top of each one. Cut out the core and increase the size of the hole using a sharp pointed knife or apple corer.

Strain the raisins and mix them with the flaked almonds, honey, cinnamon, and the reserved lemon juice and rind. Fill the apples with this mixture and put their lids back on. Set them in a buttered ovenproof dish and spread any remaining butter over each apple. Bake in the oven for about 20 minutes.

This pudding may be served warm or cold, according to taste, perhaps with a scoop of vanilla ice cream.

invite
your
mates
round

sardines on toast with a pineapple, sundried tomato and pine nut dressing

serves 4
preparation: 10 min
no cooking
refrigeration: 2hr

8 sardines in olive oil
(or the equivalent of 2 tins)
ground ginger
8 thin slices crusty bread

for the dressing
1 lime
1 teaspoon balsamic vinegar
3 tablespoons olive oil
1 slice fresh or tinned pineapple, diced
1 teaspoon diced sundried tomatoes
1 teaspoon pine kernels
1 sprig of fresh thyme
1 tablespoon mixed, roughly
chopped, fresh chives and coriander
sea salt and freshly milled pepper

Drain the sardines, put them on a plate and sprinkle a little ginger over them.

To prepare the dressing: cut a slice from the lime into very small pieces and put in a bowl with the juice of half the lime. Stir in the balsamic vinegar and olive oil and, as you mix, add the diced pineapple and sundried tomatoes, together with the pine kernels, thyme and chopped herbs.

Sprinkle this dressing over the sardines, cover and chill in the fridge for 2 hours.

Put two slices of lightly toasted bread, topped with sardines, on each plate. Cover with the remaining dressing and sprinkle over a little sea salt and freshly ground black pepper.

If you don't like the look of whole sardines, you can mash them and mix them with harissa or vinaigrette dressing. As a nice variation, you can serve the sardines on large slices of boiled potato instead of putting them on bread.

sardines on toast with harissa

serves 2
preparation: 10 min
cooking: 3 min

$\frac{1}{2}$ shallot

1 teaspoon harissa (ready prepared, in a jar or tube)

1 tablespoon olive oil

1 teaspoon mixed chopped fresh chives and coriander

1 tin sardines in oil

4 thin slices crusty bread

1 lemon

Peel and finely chop the half shallot. In a bowl, mix together the harissa, olive oil and the chopped shallot and herbs.

Drain the sardines and lightly toast the slices of bread; spread these with the harissa mixture and pop a sardine on top of each one. Arrange them on plates and sprinkle a few drops of olive oil and lemon juice over them, according to taste.

ricotta loaf with courgettes

serves 8
preparation: 30 min
cooking: 45 min

2 courgettes
2 tablespoons olive oil
1 tablespoon ground thyme
2 x 250 g/9 oz tubs ricotta
1 egg
2 tablespoons crème fraîche
3 sprigs of chives, finely chopped
salt and pepper

Preheat the oven to 190°C/375°F/Gas Mark 5.

Wash the courgettes and dice them finely. Then lightly brown them in a frying pan with 1 tablespoon of olive oil. Season and sprinkle with thyme.

Crumble the ricotta in a large bowl and then add the egg and crème fraîche and beat it all with a whisk. Stir in the courgettes and chives and mix well. Oil a cake tin, pour in the mixture and put in the oven for about 45 minutes.

Cover cakes and baked custards with a sheet of aluminium foil halfway through the cooking time, so that their tops don't burn.

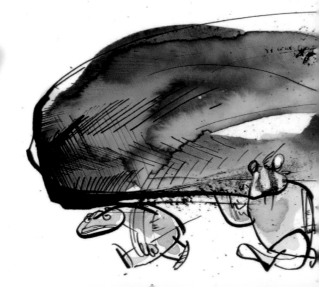

baked courgette custard

serves 8
preparation: 30 min
cooking: 40 min
refrigeration: 4 hr

1 kg/2¼ lb courgettes
2 tablespoons olive oil
2 garlic cloves, peeled and chopped
dried thyme
8 eggs
2 tablespoons crème fraîche
3 sprigs of chives, finely chopped
salt and pepper

Preheat the oven 200°C/400°F/Gas Mark 6. Wash the courgettes and cut them into dice. Then in a frying pan, heat 1 tablespoon of olive oil and brown the courgettes with the garlic. Season and sprinkle in a little thyme. Beat the eggs and crème fraîche together in a large bowl, then add the courgettes and chives and mix.

Oil a cake tin and pour in the mixture, then put it in a bain-marie *(see Glossary p. 156)* and bake in the oven for about 40 minutes. Allow to cool to room temperature before chilling in the fridge for 4 hours.

Serve accompanied by a tomato and pepper coulis *(see p. 54)*.

variation

You can also make this baked dish with a mixture of diced courgettes and red peppers.

club sandwiches

serves 4

preparation: 20 min

cooking: 10 min

small Cos or iceberg lettuce

2 tomatoes or 6 cherry tomatoes

2 tablespoons of mayonnaise

1 tablespoon of thick crème fraîche

1 teaspoon of tomato purée

1 teaspoon garlic powder

1 teaspoon of Worcestershire sauce^r

2 small chicken breasts

oil for cooking

12 slices sandwich loaf

4 slices cheese (Gruyère, Gouda, Cheddar …)

4 salami slices

salt and pepper

Wash and dry the lettuce and tomatoes then slice them thinly.

In a bowl, mix the mayonnaise, crème fraîche, tomato purée, garlic powder, Worcestershire sauce^r and salt and pepper, making sure you amalgamate them well.

Thinly slice the chicken breasts, heat the oil in a frying pan and cook the chicken for about 10 minutes. Toast the slices of bread and spread them with the mayonnaise mixture.

Spread the chicken breast and a little of the mixed lettuce and tomatoes over 4 of the slices. On another 4 slices put cheese, lettuce and tomatoes, with salami on another 4 slices.

Assemble the sandwiches by alternating a slice of bread with salami, a slice with mayonnaise only, a slice with chicken, a slice with mayonnaise only, a slice with cheese, a slice with mayonnaise only and placing them on top of each other. Repeat the process to make the second Club Sandwich.

Cut each Club Sandwich in half diagonally. Secure each triangle with a wooden skewer and serve with crisps or salad.

variation

Use salami instead of bacon: fry the bacon for 2 minutes in an oiled frying pan.

tuna in puff pastry

serves 4
preparation: 10 min
cooking: 7 min

1 onion
400 g/14 oz tinned tuna
3 tablespoons mixed chopped fresh
coriander, mint and chives
1 teaspoon ground paprika
1 teaspoon ground cumin
olive oil
4 sheets puff pastry (or filo pastry)
salt and pepper

Peel and chop the onion and soften it in a frying pan in 1 tablespoon of hot olive oil. Drain the tuna and put it in a large bowl with the onion, herbs, paprika, cumin and 1 tablespoon of olive oil. Season and mix it all together well.

Preheat the oven to 220°C/425°F/Gas Mark 7.

Brush some oil over each side of the sheets of puff pastry and cut them in half. Divide the tuna mixture between them, placing it in the centre of each half. Fold the sheets of pastry over to make a rectangle. Spread a piece of greaseproof paper on a baking sheet and place the pastry parcels on it. Cook them for about 5-7 minutes, until crispy and golden. Serve immediately with a green salad.

millefeuille of salmon and cucumber

serves 4
preparation: 10 min
no cooking

1 teaspoon horseradish cream or wasabi
1 tablespoon single cream
2 tablespoons olive oil
2 tablespoons lemon juice
1 cucumber
6 slices smoked salmon
a few chives
salt and pepper

In a bowl, mix the horseradish cream, single cream, 1 tablespoon of olive oil, lemon juice, salt and pepper.

Wash the cucumber, cut off the ends and slice it into pieces of about 10 cm/4 in. Then cut these pieces into thin slices and cut the salmon into slices of the same size.

On each plate, assemble a layered millefeuille made up of 4 slices of cucumber and 3 slices of salmon, in the following order: one cucumber slice, one salmon slice, one layer of sauce and so on, finishing with a slice of cucumber. Garnish with chives and a few drops of olive oil.

tuna fish salad

serves 4
preparation: 5 min
no cooking

400 g/14 oz tinned tuna
4 tablespoons mayonnaise
2 tablespoons chopped capers
3 sprigs of parsley, finely chopped
juice of $\frac{1}{2}$ lemon
$\frac{1}{2}$ cucumber
salt and pepper

Drain the tuna and put it in a salad bowl with the mayonnaise, capers, parsley and lemon juice. Add some pepper, and salt if required, and mash it all with a fork, mixing well. Peel, wash and cut the cucumber into small cubes and scatter them over the tuna. Serve with jacket potatoes.

quiche lorraine

serves 4–6
preparation: 5 min
cooking: 40 min

4 eggs
250 ml/9 fl oz runny crème fraîche
150 g/5 oz grated cheese
200 g/7 oz cooked ham or streaky bacon pieces
1 onion
1 garlic clove
1 bunch of chives
1 packet shortcrust pastry
salt and pepper

Preheat the oven to 200°C/400°F/Gas Mark 6. In a large bowl, beat the eggs, crème fraîche, grated cheese, salt and pepper. Cut the ham into strips. Peel and chop the onion and garlic; wash and snip the chives. Roll out the pastry and line a 20-cm quiche tin. Spread the ham, onion, garlic and chives over the pastry base and then pour the egg mixture over it. Put into the oven for 30–40 minutes. Halfway through cooking, cover the quiche with a sheet of kitchen foil to make sure it doesn't burn. You may need to reduce the oven temperature a little. Serve warm.

smoked salmon and fresh goat's cheese tart

serves 4–6
preparation: 10 min
cooking: 35 min

3 tablespoons chopped, mixed fresh coriander, dill and chives
3 tablespoons olive oil
pepper
3 slices smoked salmon
2 eggs
200 g/7 oz fresh goat's cheese
100 ml/3½ oz thick crème fraîche
1 packet flaky pastry

Preheat the oven to 200°C/400°F/Gas Mark 6. In a large bowl, make a marinade with the herbs, olive oil and pepper. Cut the salmon into large strips and put them in the marinade until later. In another bowl, mix together the eggs, goat's cheese and crème fraîche. Roll out the pastry and line a 20-cm quiche tin. Pour in the goat's cheese mixture and cook in the oven for 30 minutes. Cover with a layer of kitchen foil halfway through cooking if necessary. When cooked, scatter the strips of smoked salmon on top and serve.

spring rolls

serves 4

preparation: 30 min

no cooking

100 g/3½ oz frozen prawns, cooked
and shelled

50 g/2 oz rice vermicelli

50 g/2 oz dried shiitake mushrooms

½ cucumber

16 fresh mint leaves

100 g/3½ oz soya bean sprouts

100 g/3½ oz Chinese cabbage

1 shallot

8 rice sheets (from Chinese
supermarkets)

1 grated carrot

Spring rolls can be enjoyed just as they are or covered in a dressing made of Nuoc Mam fish sauce and soy sauce, to which you can add lemon juice, garlic and chilli powder.

Rinse the prawns under hot water to thaw them, then drain and reserve.

Put the vermicelli and the mushrooms separately into a bowl of boiling water. When the vermicelli is soft, drain and cut the strands into halves. After 15 minutes, drain the mushrooms and cut them into very fine strips. Wash the cucumber without peeling it. Cut it in half lengthways, remove the seeds and cut it into 8 short sticks. Wash and drain the mint leaves and bean sprouts and chop both the cabbage and shallot finely.

Place the rice sheets, one by one, in a bowl of hot water for about 1 minute, to soften them slightly. Spread them out on a board and wipe with absorbent kitchen paper if necessary. Divide all the ingredients equally between the rice sheets, without forgetting the grated carrot, cabbage, shallot and cucumber, placing the mixture in the centre of each one. Fold in the shorter sides of each sheet and then roll it up. Place two spring rolls on each plate.

lemon-flavoured olive cake

serves 6
preparation: 15 min
cooking: 45 min

125 g/4½ oz butter, melted (or the equivalent in olive oil)

rind of 2 lemons

250 g/9 oz plain flour

3 teaspoons baking powder

1 teaspoon salt

3 eggs

200 g/7 oz stoned olives (black or green)

2 teaspoons mixed rosemary and thyme (fresh or dried)

Preheat the oven to 200°C/400°F/Gas Mark 6.

Grease a cake tin. Scrub the lemon rind and remove the pith, then cut the rind into narrow strips and chop finely. Sift the flour, baking powder and salt into a large bowl, make a well in the centre and pour in the melted butter. Mix well, then fold in the eggs one by one. Adding the olives, lemon rind and mixed herbs. Put the mixture into the prepared cake tin, smooth the top and bake for about 45 minutes. Test by inserting a metal skewer. If it comes out wet, bake for a little longer.

variations

Bacon and olive cake: halve the amount of olives and replace the lemon rind with 100 g/3½ oz chopped streaky bacon. Serve with tomato and red pepper coulis *(see recipe p. 54).*

Carrot and almond cake: replace the olives and lemon rind with 400 g/14 oz grated carrot, 1 teaspoon ground cinnamon, 1 teaspoon nutmeg and 100 g/3½ oz flaked almonds.

Cherry cake with candied lemon peel: replace the olives and lemon peel with 125 g/4 oz glace cherries, 125 g/4 oz candied lemon peel and 100 g/3½ oz flaked almonds or raisins. Add 125 g/4 oz caster sugar and use butter, not oil.

spanish gazpacho

serves 4
preparation: 10 min
no cooking
refrigeration: 8 hr

1 kg/2¼ lb tomatoes
1 cucumber
1 red pepper
1 onion
1 garlic clove
1 small tin tomato purée
3 tablespoons olive oil
juice of 1 lemon
1 mint sprig
salt and pepper

Skin the tomatoes *(see p. 50)*, cut in half and remove the seeds. Peel the cucumber, cut in half lengthways and remove the seeds. Wash the pepper, cut in half and remove the seeds and pith. Peel and finely chop the onion and garlic. Cut the pepper and cucumber into small pieces and put half of them in the bowl of a liquidiser. Add the onion and garlic, the tomatoes, 25 g/1 oz of tomato purée, and the olive oil and lemon juice. Season and liquidise all the ingredients. (Finely dice the remaining pepper and cucumber, put in a bowl covered with clingfilm, and place in the fridge.) Refrigerate the gazpacho for 8 hours. Before serving, put the diced pepper and cucumber into a large bowl, stir in the gazpacho and check the seasoning. Garnish with a sprig of mint.
Serve with a bowl of croutons, either plain or rubbed with garlic.

variation
Mexican gazpacho: Add 2 teaspoons of chilli powder and, before serving, stir in the flesh of 2 avocados, cut into large dice. Adjust the chilli powder seasoning and serve accompanied by a bowl of guacamole and a bowl of salsa *(see recipe p. 127)*.

If the gazpacho seems too thick, add a little water. If, on the other hand, it's too runny, mix in some tomato purée.

tofu with coconut milk

serves 4

preparation: 10 min

cooking: 15 min

1 shallot

1 tablespoon olive oil

500 ml/18 fl oz chicken stock

500 ml/18 fl oz coconut milk

3 tablespoons soy sauce

juice of $\frac{1}{2}$ lime

1 tablespoon ground ginger

1 pinch of chilli powder (or 2 drops of Tabasco®)

600 g/1 lb 5 oz tofu

1 tablespoon finely chopped fresh coriander

salt and pepper

Peel and slice the shallot very thinly. Heat the oil in a frying pan and soften the shallot, then remove from the pan and drain on kitchen paper. Pour the chicken stock, coconut milk, soy sauce and lime juice into a large saucepan and add the shallot, ginger and chilli (or Tabasco®). Season and cook for about 15 minutes over a medium heat, stirring often.

Strain the tofu and cut into cubes. Divide it between four bowls, with the coriander, and pour the coconut milk broth over it. Leave to infuse for 2 minutes before serving.

sweetcorn pancakes

serves 4
preparation: 10 min
cooking: 15 min
standing time: 20 min
280 g/10 oz tin sweetcorn
3 eggs
85 g/3 oz yellow cornmeal
2 tablespoons milk
groundnut oil
salt

Drain the sweetcorn and put two-thirds of it into a large bowl, with the eggs, cornmeal, milk and 2 pinches of salt. Mix it together and leave to stand for 20 minutes. Then mix with the remaining sweetcorn.

Heat the oil in a frying pan and fry small ladlefuls of the batter. When the pancakes are nice and golden on both sides, lift them out on to absorbent kitchen paper.

Serve 2 pancakes on each plate with a fried chicken leg or breast in mole poblano sauce.

mole poblano (chocolate and chilli sauce)

for 1 bowl
preparation: 10 min
cooking: 1 hr
1 garlic clove
1 tomato
1 green chilli
2 tablespoons unsweetened cocoa powder
200 ml/7 fl oz chicken stock
1/2 tortilla (or a slice of bread)
1 teaspoon sesame seeds
1 teaspoon ground coriander
oil for cooking
salt

Peel and chop the garlic and wash and skin the tomato. Cut the chilli in half, remove the seeds, rinse it under hot water, then dry it and cut into small pieces. Put all the ingredients, except for the cooking oil, together with 2 pinches of salt into the mixer bowl of a food processor and grind until they form a paste.

Put the oil in a saucepan to heat; then pour in the mixture and let it cook for 1 hour over a low heat, stirring often.

Serve as an accompaniment to the sweetcorn pancakes.

prawn curry

serves 6
preparation: 15 min
cooking: 10 min

800 g/1¾ lb, fresh or frozen prawns,
cooked and shelled
2 tomatoes
1 tablespoon olive oil
1 tablespoon red curry paste or
powder
100 g/3½ oz tinned bamboo shoots,
drained
300 ml/10 fl oz coconut milk
juice of 1 lime
1 teaspoon garlic powder
for garnish: a few fresh green beans
and soya bean sprouts
salt and pepper

Dear Mum,
Instead of prawns, I used thinly
sliced chicken. A chicken curry's
not bad with rice!
A lamb or aubergine curry goes
better with Cucumber Raïta.

If using frozen prawns, ensure that they are
thoroughly defrosted.
Wash the tomatoes and cut them into small
pieces.
Heat the oil in a frying pan and add the curry
paste (or powder). Add the tomatoes and
cook for 3 minutes. Then mix in the prawns,
bamboo shoots, coconut milk and lime juice.
Stir in the garlic powder and season, then
leave to cook for 7 minutes over a low heat.
Serve in individual bowls or from a deep dish,
garnished with a few cooked green beans and
soya bean sprouts, and accompanied by flavoured rice.

chicken fajitas

serves 4
preparation: 45 min
marinade: 4 hr
cooking: 15 min

3 chicken breasts
2 green peppers
1 red pepper
1 onion
1 tablespoon olive oil

for the marinade
1 tablespoon garlic powder
1 tablespoon onion powder
2 tablespoons olive oil
3 drops of Tabasco®
pepper

to serve
1 bowl each of guacamole
and salsa *(see opposite)*
1 bowl of fromage frais
8 corn tortillas

To prepare the marinade: Mix all the ingredients in a bowl.

Cut the chicken breasts into slices and add to the marinade, cover with clingfilm and leave to marinate in the fridge for 4 hours. (Remove them from the fridge while you're preparing the other ingredients, to give them time to return to room temperature.) Wash the peppers, cut them in half and remove the seeds and pith. Peel the onion and then cut both peppers and onion into fine strips.

Heat the olive oil in a frying pan and brown the chicken. Then add the vegetables and the liquid from the marinade. Continue cooking over a medium heat until all the ingredients are soft. Serve accompanied by guacamole, salsa, fromage frais and piping hot tortillas. Your guests can all make their own fajitas by wrapping a little of each ingredient in the tortillas.

salsa

makes 1 bowl
preparation: 10 min
no cooking

2 tomatoes, $\frac{1}{2}$ red pepper
1 tablespoon tomato purée
1 teaspoon garlic powder
1 teaspoon onion powder
6 drops of Tabasco®
3 tablespoons olive oil
juice of 2 limes
salt and pepper

Skin the tomatoes *(see p. 50)* and wash the red pepper. Finely dice the tomatoes and pepper, then put them in a bowl with all the other ingredients except the salt and pepper, which should be added, to taste, at the end. Mix well and store in a cool place.

guacamole

Peel and finely chop the garlic and onion. Put into a bowl and mix with the tomato purée, crushed chilli, coriander, turmeric, olive oil, lemon juice, salt and pepper.
Cut the avocados in half and discard the stone. Put the flesh into a bowl and mash with a fork until you have a purée. Add to the bowl of flavourings and mix well. Check the seasoning and chill, covered, until ready to serve.

makes 1 bowl
preparation: 5 min
no cooking

1 garlic clove
1 onion
1 tablespoon tomato purée
1 small dried chilli
1 pinch of ground coriander
1 pinch of ground turmeric
2 tablespoons olive oil
juice of 1 lemon
2 ripe avocados
salt and pepper

127

tandoori chicken

serves 4
preparation: 10 min
marinade: 4 hr
cooking: 30 min

4 chicken legs
250 g/9 oz plain yogurt
juice of $\frac{1}{2}$ lemon
3 tablespoons tandoori powder or paste
1 tablespoon garlic powder
1 tablespoon ground ginger
2 tablespoons groundnut oil
1 teaspoon ground black pepper

Remove the skin from the chicken legs. Put the yogurt in a bowl and add the lemon juice, spices and some pepper, then spread this mixture over the chicken legs, cover with clingfilm and leave to marinate for 4 hours in the fridge. Put the chicken legs on an oiled baking tray and cook under the grill for 30 minutes. Pierce deeply with a skewer to ensure that the juices are clear. Serve with naan bread and rice.

chicken kebabs with ginger and sesame seeds

serves 4
preparation: 10 min
cooking: 15 min

2 tablespoons soy sauce
3 tablespoons sesame seeds
4 chicken breasts
1 knob of butter
1 teaspoon groundnut oil
2 tablespoons ground ginger
juice of $\frac{1}{2}$ lime
a few chives, finely snipped
salt and pepper

Put the soy sauce in a bowl with 1 teaspoon of the sesame seeds. Spread the rest of the sesame seeds on to a plate. Cut the chicken breasts into large cubes. Combine the butter and oil in a frying pan and put the chicken to brown in the pan over a high heat, stirring constantly. After about 5 minutes, sprinkle over the ginger and some grinds of the peppermill. Stir and continue cooking for 4–5 minutes over a medium heat, then remove the chicken pieces to a plate and keep warm.

Deglaze the pan over a moderate heat by adding the lime juice and scraping at the base to gather in all the tasty bits and juices, then add the chives and stir it all into the soy and sesame seed sauce.

Add a little salt to the chicken and make 4 or 8 kebabs by threading the chicken pieces on to skewers. Roll the kebabs in the sesame seeds. Serve the kebabs covered with the sauce and with tofu as an accompaniment.

chilli con carne

serves 4
preparation: 10 min
cooking: 1 hr

2 onions

1 garlic clove

1 green pepper

2 tablespoons oil

450 g/1 lb minced beef

1 tablespoon chilli powder

1 small dried Cayenne pepper (optional)

400 g/14 oz tin peeled, chopped tomatoes

small tin tomato purée

1 large tin red kidney beans

8 oz basmati rice

salt

Peel and chop the onions and garlic. Wash the pepper, deseed and discard the pith, then cut into small dice. Heat the oil in a pan and soften the onions and garlic. Add the diced pepper. Continue cooking for about 2–3 minutes, then add the mince to brown. You will need to keep stirring and turning it. When it has all browned, add the chilli powder and crushed dried pepper (if using), pour in the tomatoes and tomato purée, and the red kidney beans with their juice. Add some salt, mix well, cover and leave to simmer for 1 hour. About 20 minutes before serving, cook the rice in a large saucepan of salted boiling water. Lay the rice in a circle on the serving dish and put the chilli in the centre of it.

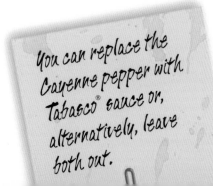

You can replace the Cayenne pepper with Tabasco® sauce or, alternatively, leave both out.

chocolate cookies

makes 20 cookies
preparation: 15 min
cooking: 15 min

250 g/9 oz dark chocolate
250 g/9 oz plain flour
1½ teaspoons baking powder
2 eggs
250 g/9 oz softened butter
200 g/7 oz caster sugar
vanilla extract

Preheat the oven to 200°C/400°F/Gas Mark 6. Melt the dark chocolate in a bowl set over a saucepan of barely simmering water. The bowl mustn't touch the water.

Sift the flour and baking powder into a bowl and make a well in the centre. Add the eggs and beat to a smooth batter, then set aside to rest.

In another bowl whisk the butter, caster sugar and a few drops of vanilla extract until you have a creamy mixture, pour this mixture into the bowl containing the batter and then add the chocolate. Whisk it all together to give a light texture.

Put 3 or 4 sheets of greaseproof paper on a baking tray and spoon on 20 blobs of mixture. Flatten with a fork, leaving space between each cookie – you may need 2 trays. Bake for a maximum of 15 minutes. Carefully take the cookies off the tray with a spatula. Serve hot or cold, with ice cream perhaps?

Cookies and brownies
For more flavour, add 200 g/7 oz of chocolate chips to the chocolate mixture, and some chopped pecan nuts, hazel nuts, almonds, pistachios, or shredded coconut.
White chocolate instead of dark would be different!

brownies

serves 12
preparation: 15 min
cooking: 45 min
250 g/9 oz dark chocolate
250 g/9 oz butter
150 g/5 oz plain flour
1½ teaspoons baking powder
3 eggs
300 g/10 oz caster sugar
vanilla extract

Preheat the oven to 200°C/400°F/Gas Mark 6. Melt the chocolate and butter in a saucepan over a very low heat, then leave to cool. Sift the flour and baking powder into a large bowl. Mix in each egg, then the sugar and a few drops of vanilla extract. Add the cooled chocolate mixture. Butter a rectangular cake tin, spread the cake mixture in it and bake for 15–20 minutes, then cover with aluminium foil and continue baking for another 15 minutes. Cut into 12 slices.

tiramisu

serves 6
preparation: 15 min
refrigeration: 2 hr
2 x 250 g/9 oz tubs mascarpone
100 ml/3½ fl oz single cream
3 egg yolks
100 g/3½ oz caster sugar
1 teaspoon vanilla extract
24 sponge finger biscuits
300 ml/½ pint espresso
cocoa powder

Mix the mascarpone and single cream together in a large bowl. In another bowl, beat the egg yolks with the sugar and vanilla extract. Add to the mascarpone mixture and beat again. Pour half the mixture into a serving dish, then quickly dip each sponge finger in the coffee and arrange on top. Cover with the rest of the mascarpone and refrigerate for 2 hours. Dust with cocoa powder just before serving.

apple crumble

serves 4
preparation: 15 min
cooking: 35 min

for the apple mixture
4 large cooking apples
1 knob of butter
juice of $\frac{1}{2}$ lemon
1 tablespoon caster sugar
1 teaspoon ground cinnamon

for the topping
100 g/3$\frac{1}{2}$ oz plain flour
70 g/2$\frac{1}{2}$ oz butter, cut into pieces
75 g/3 oz caster sugar
salt

To prepare the apples: Peel and core the apples, cut into pieces and place in a buttered gratin dish. Sprinkle the lemon juice on top, followed by the sugar and cinnamon.

Preheat the oven to 220°C/425°F/Gas Mark 7.
To prepare the topping: Sift the flour and a pinch of salt into a large bowl and add the butter and sugar. Crumble it all together using two forks, or your fingertips, so that it looks like breadcrumbs. Scatter it over the apples. Put in the oven for about 35 minutes, until the top is nice and golden.
This should be eaten as soon as it comes out of the oven, with thick crème fraîche or vanilla ice cream.

tip
You can add raisins to the apples, or blueberries or stewed rhubarb.
Or the crumble can be made using red berries and currants, or a mixture of mango and peaches.

talking of fruit coulis

You can make a coulis using different fruits by just mixing the washed and prepared fruit together. Berry fruits can be pushed through a nylon-mesh sieve with the back of a wooden spoon. Other fruits (peeled and stoned, if necessary) may need a whizz in the liquidiser, then passed through the sieve to remove pips and seeds.

red berry coulis with ginger

mix together 450 g/1 lb of fresh or frozen red berries (strawberries, rasp-berries, cherries, redcurrants, etc.), 2 tablespoons of caster sugar and 1 teaspoon of ground ginger.

peach, melon and fresh mint coulis

mix together 4 peaches (2 white, 2 yellow), 1 small melon, 6 fresh mint leaves and sugar to taste.

exotic fruit coulis

mix together 1 mango, 200 g/7 oz passion fruit, 1 orange and sugar to taste.

panna cotta with fruit coulis

serves 6
preparation: 15 min
cooking: 7 min
refrigeration: 12 hr

1½ sachets of powdered gelatine
1 litre/1¾ pints single cream
150 g/5 oz caster sugar
1 vanilla pod

Dissolve the powdered gelatine as instructed on the packet (or use 5 gelatine leaves, softened).

Put the cream and sugar into a saucepan, split the vanilla pod in two and scrape the seeds into the pan.

Cook over a low heat, stirring often (the cream should just simmer and mustn't boil). After 7 minutes, draw the cream off the heat and take out the vanilla pod. Stir the gelatine into the hot cream, stirring until completely dissolved. Pour the mixture into a buttered cake tin and place in the fridge for 12 hours. Turn out onto a dessert plate and serve with a fruit coulis *(see recipes opposite)*.

variation
For *milk chocolate panna cotta*, just add 175 g/ 6 oz of melted milk chocolate and reduce the quantity of sugar to 75 g/3 oz.

Dear Mum,
I've tried the panna cotta with caramel made with salted butter. I've also served it with pieces of candied fruit (melon, apricot, orange and lemon peel).

for you, MUM

It's Sunday, it's getting late but we don't want to break up the party. None of us has noticed the time, we've been so engrossed in playing cards. The only food shop open at night is at the other end of town – a real hassle to go and buy stuff. On the other hand, just to go out for a snack leaving John the pleasure of having won – no way. The fight's not over yet.

We pause between two rounds and I retreat to my headquarters: two square metres of kitchen. My only cupboard and my fridge stand to attention, displaying their artillery for my inspection: rice, a packet of peanuts, a tin of peeled tomatoes, a chorizo with one end missing, plain tuna and some strawberries. Total luxury! 'Hey lads, help me peel some onion and garlic and open some tins. I'm going to make you some rice. You can hull some strawberries too, while you're at it!'

John went white – he was counting on the fact that we were famished to get away with winning.

In two seconds flat, I'd put on my apron and got out the frying pan, ready to launch the counter-attack. And sure enough, once we'd satisfied our hunger, Henri, Louis and I managed to thrash John.

As we were saying goodbye at the door, John said: 'We can play another game to decide who wins whenever you want, especially if you do the meal again'.

That night John, the bad loser who hated not winning, went off without complaining. My rice concoction had got the better of him and the *strawberries in balsamic vinegar* had added to the surprise effect. He admitted having lost the battle, but not the war. We'd have another game soon.

I had changed the course of events with my act of culinary hero-ism! My little contribution had brought us all closer. Thanks to you, Mum – your words stick in my mind: 'Give pleasure to those you love: you can do it with next to nothing, nothing at all. Think of cooking. That's what it's there for'. It took a lot of trial and error before I could really understand what you meant about making do whith what I had.

I didn't have the nerve to cook, still less to improvise. You should have seen me at the beginning! I felt like a castaway, all at sea. I rationed myself to survive (fortunately, I didn't have much appetite away from home for the first time).

Your bagful of goodies lasted more than a week but, after nibbling away at it for the hundredth time, it was desperately empty. Or almost empty – there were six eggs left. I had put off the moment of cooking them, I'd even banished the word cooking from my vocabulary. You were the only one who could cook for me and concoct nice little recipes – and you weren't there to feed me. Those eggs didn't interest me, and hard-boiling them or frying them or making them into an omelette with nothing else to go with them was not remotely tempting. You know how I love food! I read your notebook again and again to try to dig up some ideas, but without success – it seemed off limits. You were the sole owner; the recipes and ideas you'd written down in it were yours by right, and I had no right to touch them.

Those eggs were beginning to depress me. I cursed them, but couldn't bring myself to throw them away.

A few days before their expiry date, I remembered one of grandma's sayings: 'You must never waste food,' and it really got to me.

The countdown to getting rid of them was hanging over me like a judgement. I was guilty. But finding a way of adapting them as quickly as possible might save me! And so I went off to replenish the store cupboard for my six eggs.

Just as you took over grandma's saying, Mum, I adopted it too: I repeated it like a mantra all the way to the market: 'You must never waste food', 'You must never waste food', 'You must never waste food' … And then I filled up the shopping bag you gave me.

I'll always remember my first experience of shopping. I had a bunch of radishes and a bunch of sweet-smelling basil, some minced steak and some chicken breast. The woman who sold me some vegetables and two bananas gave me two lemons as well, and a mixture of herbs wrapped in a piece of faded blue paper. I was touched on behalf of my six eggs. Watching you thousands of times in the kitchen helped me to know what I was doing and there were some things I knew instinctively. I moved from theory to practice via my guilt trip.

I put an egg on to hard-boil in a saucepan and sliced the radishes, then I combined them to make a *carpaccio of radishes with hard-boiled egg*. Then I made an omelette from the stalks of the radishes and two beaten eggs. With the minced steak, an egg and some rusk I made *meat balls and soya bean sprouts*.

I had some chicken stock left over from my poached *chicken breast and couscous*, so I turned that into a chicken broth with milk and egg. Then I fried the last two eggs to go with my delicious sautéed vegetables.

I mixed the half bunch of basil I hadn't used with some olive oil and garlic to flavour my spaghetti. And I baked my bananas in butter, sugar and lemon juice, before rolling them in shredded coconut. These two recipes didn't need any eggs. All the trouble I'd taken to save them from the dustbin had given me a feeling of liberation: although it had started out being a duty I'd ended up cooking for pleasure. I kept the egg box as a sign of victory! I read your notebook differently then, and saw it as 'the world I had to conquer'. You told me to 'create my own universe'. So now your notebook really belongs to me. I recreate your recipes and I've even improved on some of them.

I've made up menus and I invite my friends round to chill out over a good meal. I'm no longer a castaway; I've reached dry land. I feel at home in the town I'm living in. Oh, and I've just met a girl called Elisa. She's coming round to dinner tonight.

To Elisa

My heart is struck like a match alight.
For Elisa is dining with me tonight.
And for this dinner for two we have:
Roquefort crackers and mashed bananas with tomato, passata
Prawn kebabs with ginger and lime
Tomatoes bursting with butter caramel and toasted nuts.

My heart is struck like a match alight.
I've written the menu as Christian might —
My godfather Christian, who didn't fail
To send the dessert recipe by email.
The crackers are an improvisation,
the rice and kebabs an invention.

My heart is struck like a match alight
As I make sure the candles burn bright,
Ready to welcome you here.
My voice quivers, betraying me all the while,
At its notes high and low I cannot but smile.

My heart is struck like a match alight.
The sensations I feel are real all right.

My heart is struck like a match alight
As I think of the laughs we'll share tonight.
But matches can only be struck once, and
no more
And, dear Elisa, I've been struck by you,
for sure.

roquefort crackers and mashed banana with tomato passata

serves 2

preparation: 5 min

cooking: 2 min

2 knobs of butter

50 g/2 oz Roquefort

2 cherry tomatoes

$\frac{1}{2}$ banana

2 large or 4 small crackers

1 sprig of thyme, or a pinch of dried

olive oil

a few salad leaves

salt and pepper

Put a knob of butter in a saucepan with the Roquefort and some pepper. Stir while it melts and then put to one side.

Wash the cherry tomatoes and cut them into very small pieces. Fry the mashed banana in a knob of butter and add salt and pepper.

Spread the crackers with three-quarters of the melted Roquefort and put the banana on top, then spread the remaining Roquefort over this. Garnish with the tomato pieces and thyme. Finish with a few drops of olive oil.

Serve on Cos lettuce leaves or other greenery, but do serve immediately to keep the crunchiness.

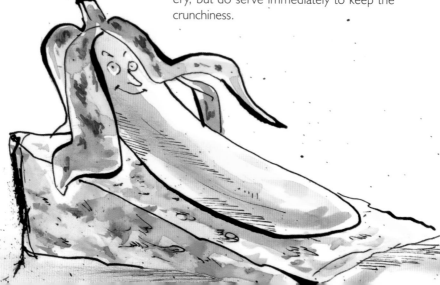

carpaccio of radishes with hard-boiled egg

serves 1
preparation: 10 min
no cooking
$\frac{1}{2}$ bunch of fresh basil, finely chopped
1 tablespoon olive oil
1 teaspoon balsamic vinegar
1 tablespoon lemon juice
1 bunch of radishes
1 hard-boiled egg, chopped
salt and pepper

Prepare the dressing in a bowl by mixing together the basil, olive oil, balsamic vinegar, lemon juice, salt and pepper.

Wash and dry the radishes after having removed their tops and stalks. Then cut them into fine, almost translucent, slices. Arrange them on a flat plate and sprinkle the dressing over them, followed by the chopped hard-boiled egg.

omelette with radish stalks

serves 1
preparation: 10 min
cooking: 10 min
the stalks from a bunch of radishes, washed and finely chopped
1 tablespoon oil (or 1 knob of butter)
1 teaspoon onion powder
1 teaspoon garlic powder
2 eggs
salt and pepper

Fry the radish stalks in oil or butter until the water in them evaporates and they become soft. Sprinkle the radish stalks with the onion and garlic powder, salt and pepper.

Whisk the eggs in a large bowl and pour them over the stalks. Leave to cook until the base of the omelette is firm but, while the eggs are still moist, fold one side of the omelette over on to the other using a spatula.

Serve straight away with ham or with a piece of Emmenthal or Gruyère cheese.

rice with tuna, chorizo and peanuts

Drain the tuna, then wash the lemon and cut into four. Peel the onion and cut into strips, then peel and chop the garlic cloves. Remove the skin from the chorizo and slice it thinly.

Heat a lightly oiled frying pan and brown the chorizo, then take it out and leave on a plate. Now brown the peanuts. Transfer them to a plate and do the same with the tuna. Put everything to one side.

Soften the onion and garlic and add the tomatoes. Let them reduce for 3 minutes, then remove them from the pan to a plate.

Put the rice into the frying pan and let it brown, then cover it with water. After 2 minutes, sprinkle in some salt and pepper, saffron and the crushed chilli pepper. Leave to simmer until the rice has absorbed all the liquid. Before it has finished cooking, when the rice is still a little firm, add the tomato and onion mixture, with any juices, followed by the tuna. Stir and, if necessary, adjust the seasoning and add a little water to continue cooking the rice.

Garnish with the chorizo, peanuts and lemon pieces. Serve directly from the frying pan.

serves 4
preparation: 10 min
cooking: 35 min

280 g/10 oz tinned tuna
1 untreated or well-scrubbed lemon
1 large onion
2 garlic cloves
1 mild chorizo
2 handfuls of peanuts
400 g/14 oz tin peeled plum tomatoes
300 g/10 oz rice
600 ml/1 pint water
1 teaspoon saffron powder
1 dried chilli pepper, crushed
salt and pepper

meat balls and soya bean sprouts

serves 1
preparation: 10 min
cooking: 7 min

1 rusk
150 g/5 oz steak mince
1 egg
1 teaspoon ground cumin
1 teaspoon Worcestershire sauce®
1 tablespoon oil for cooking
100 g/3½ oz soya bean sprouts,
washed and drained
1 tablespoon soy sauce
3 sprigs of coriander, finely chopped
pepper

In a large bowl, crumble the rusk then add the meat, egg, cumin, Worcestershire sauce®, and pepper. Mix it all together well and shape into 4 small balls.

Heat 1 tablespoon of oil in a frying pan and put the meat balls in to brown for 2 minutes over a high heat. Lower the heat to medium and add the soya bean sprouts. Continue cooking for 4 minutes so that the bean sprouts are half cooked.

Before serving, sprinkle with soy sauce and coriander.

spaghetti with garlic and basil

serves 1
preparation: 5 min
cooking: 10 min

100 g/3½ oz spaghetti
1 tablespoon olive oil
1–2 teaspoons garlic powder,
according to taste
½ bunch of fresh basil, chopped
freshly grated Parmesan
salt and pepper

Cook the spaghetti until it is *al dente*.

Then, in a bowl, mix together the olive oil, garlic, basil, salt and pepper.

Drain the spaghetti, transfer it to a serving dish and pour the garlic and basil sauce over it. Sprinkle the grated Parmesan over the top.

tip
Finely chopped cherry tomatoes or red pepper bring a note of colour and some different flavours.

pan of mixed vegetables

serves 2
preparation: 10 min
cooking: 3-5 min for each
vegetable

1 carrot
2 large button, or closed white
mushrooms
1 head of broccoli
1 courgette
oil for cooking
1 tablespoon onion powder
1 teaspoon ground ginger
soy sauce
1 tablespoon fresh, finely chopped,
mixed herbs of your choice
salt and pepper

Peel the carrot and wipe the mushrooms. Wash the remaining vegetables: remove the stalk from the broccoli and separate the florets, slice the mushrooms, cut the courgette into batons and dice the carrot. Heat a little oil in a frying pan or wok and stir-fry all the vegetables separately, starting with the broccoli (which takes longest to cook). They should all remain slightly crunchy. Add some more oil between batches if necessary.

Return all the vegetables to the pan and sprinkle over the onion powder, ginger, 1 tablespoon of soy sauce and some pepper. Add salt if necessary and simmer for 2 minutes over a low heat. Before serving, sprinkle over the chopped herbs and flavour with soy sauce. This is good eaten with fried eggs.

Dear Mum,
There are endless variations on this pan
of mixed vegetables – it's easy.
You can mix:
– broad beans, peas and green beans;
– soya bean sprouts, bamboo shoots and
carrots;
– mushrooms and carrots;
– potatoes, carrots and mushrooms;
– broccoli, green beans and bamboo shoots.

chicken breast and couscous with capers and almonds

serves 1
preparation: 10 min
cooking: 15 min

1 cm/$\frac{1}{2}$ inch lemon peel, finely chopped

1 shallot

3 crushed peppercorns

1 teaspoon garlic powder

1 litre/1$\frac{3}{4}$ pints chicken stock

1 chicken breast

1 cm/$\frac{1}{2}$ inch fresh ginger, finely chopped

olive oil

100 g/3$\frac{1}{2}$ oz couscous

2 teaspoons flaked almonds

1 teaspoon capers

1 sprig chive

salt

Chop the lemon peel finely, peel the shallot and cut it into thin slices, then put these to one side.

Put the peppercorns, garlic and chicken stock in a saucepan and bring to the boil. Remove from the heat, cover and leave to infuse for 5 minutes. Place the chicken breast in the stock, return the pan to the hob and let it cook for 10 minutes over a low heat, then remove from the heat and take out 1 cup of stock. Cover the pan so that the chicken stays hot.

Soften the ginger, lemon peel and shallot in a frying pan containing a little olive oil, then put the couscous on top and cook it slightly before pouring over half a cup of stock. Add salt and stir, then take it off the heat to allow it to swell. Fluff it up with a fork to separate the grains. Top up with stock or finish cooking over the heat as necessary. Add the almonds and capers and mix again.

Serve the couscous in a bowl, with the chicken in a deep dish, covered with a little stock and garnished with snipped chives.

tip

With the unused stock, you can make egg nog for the evening (see recipe opposite).

egg nog

serves 1
preparation: 5 min
cooking: 15 min

1 egg
200 ml/7 fl oz milk
the remains of the stock from the
previous recipe
salt and pepper

Separate the egg white from the yolk, and reserve the white. Whisk the egg yolk with the milk.

Put the rest of the stock in a saucepan and add the milk and egg yolk, mixing well, then add salt and pepper. Heat this mixture over a low heat, stirring continuously to bind it and make it thicken. Then slide the egg white down the side of the saucepan and, using a fork, whisk it quickly so that it forms strings.

Serve with toasted croutons.

tip

The addition of some vermicelli gives an extra touch of style to the presentation of the egg nog.

prawn kebabs with ginger and lime

Wash 1 lime, cut it into cubes and reserve. Wash the red pepper, remove the seeds and pith and cut into small dice. Sauté briefly in a frying pan with 1 tablespoon of olive oil. Remove from the pan to a plate and season to taste. Carefully shell the prawns, removing their heads and tails to detach the body. Slit the back and remove the black thread. Put the prawns into a bowl mixed with the turmeric, ginger, chives and the juice from the second lime.

Cook the rice as indicated on the packet and keep warm. Drain the prawns, reserving the marinade. Put 1 tablespoon of olive oil into a hot frying pan and cook the prawns for 2 minutes over a high heat, then reduce the heat and cook for 2 minutes. Sprinkle the prawn tails with the marinade, stir and allow it to evaporate for a few seconds. Pour the prawn cooking juices into a bowl with the soy sauce and sesame seeds.

Thread a piece of lime, a prawn, a piece of lime, and so on to 6 wooden skewers. Shape the basmati rice into 4 little stick shapes. Present the kebabs in a large dish, sprinkled with a few drops of the sesame sauce, and the rice sticks covered with the diced peppers. Serve with the bowl of sauce.

serves 2
preparation: 15 min
cooking: 8 min

2 limes
1 red pepper
2 tablespoons olive oil
6 large unshelled, uncooked prawns, (jumbo, tiger, etc.)
1 teaspoon ground turmeric
2 teaspoons ground ginger
6 chives
125 g/4 oz basmati rice
4 tablespoons soy sauce
sesame seeds
salt and pepper

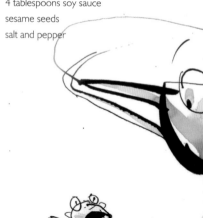

tomatoes bursting with butter caramel and toasted nuts

serves 2
preparation: 15 min
cooking: 15 min

2 large tomatoes
100 g/3½ oz caster sugar
25 g/1 oz butter
100 ml/3½ fl oz single cream
30 g/1 oz green walnuts
30 g/1 oz flaked almonds
30 g/1 oz pistachio nuts
30 g/1 oz pine nuts

Wash and peel the tomatoes, cut little lids from the tops, scoop out the seeds, and leave to drain upside down.

Put the sugar in a saucepan and heat over gently, stirring constantly. When it has turned a dark caramel colour, it is ready. Take it off the heat and add the butter and single cream. Mix well.

Toast the nuts for a few seconds in the frying pan then add them to the caramel. Fill the tomatoes with this mixture and put their lids back on prior to serving.

tip
This tomato dessert may be accompanied by an apricot coulis with olive oil or orange juice *(see coulis recipes p. 136)*.

153

strawberries in balsamic vinegar syrup

serves 4
preparation: 10 min
cooking: 10 min
marinade: 30 min

450 g/1 lb strawberries
100 g/3½ oz caster sugar
1 clove
200 ml/7 fl oz water
3 tablespoons balsamic vinegar
strips of zest pared from 1 lemon

Rinse and hull the strawberries, then cut them in half and put them in a large bowl.

In a saucepan, mix the sugar and clove with the water and bring to the boil. Remove the pan from the heat and leave to infuse for 5 minutes. Then add the balsamic vinegar, stir and leave the syrup to go cold. Pour it over the strawberries and marinate for 30 minutes. Fish out the clove and then decorate with lemon zest. Serve with lime ice cream, or your favourite topping.

coconut bananas

serves 2
preparation: 5 min
cooking: 10 min

1 knob of butter
2 bananas
1–2 tablespoons caster sugar
1 teaspoon grated fresh ginger
juice from ½ lemon
desiccated coconut

Melt the butter in a frying pan over a medium heat and add the peeled bananas. After 5 minutes, sprinkle the sugar and ginger over them. Turn the heat down low and cook the bananas on both sides, turning them with the help of two wooden spatulas. Sprinkle over the lemon juice halfway through the cooking. The bananas are ready when they are melting and caramelised.

Before serving, roll the bananas (carefully so as not to break them) in the coconut.

glossary

al dente (literally 'to the tooth') the cooking time, which varies according to the type of pasta, is short enough for the pasta to have some 'bite' in it. It must not overcook or it becomes tasteless and sticky.

bain-marie a bowl or basin, filled with a mixture to be melted or gently heated, is placed inside another receptacle, often a roasting tin, containing boiling water.

balsamic vinegar is a speciality of Modena (Italy) and is obtained from grape must (unfermented juice), which is aged in wooden casks. The longer the period of ageing, the higher the quality of the vinegar produced.

basil an aromatic herb that is essential in Italian cooking. It is used, preferably fresh, to flavour oil, pasta, fish and meat. Thai basil has a milder flavour.

Coriander aromatic plant originally from Asia or North Africa.

Couscous fine, medium or coarse grains of wheat semolina used for making *couscous*, a traditional North African dish based on meat or fish and vegetables. Couscous can also be used for making sweet dishes.

Curry can be strong or mild and comes as a powder or paste. The most highly spiced ones contain a mixture of turmeric, cloves, cardamom, cumin, paprika, nutmeg, cinnamon and hot peppers. Serves to enhance dishes and give them piquancy.

deglaze to retrieve the caramelised cooking juices and browned bits left at the bottom of a pan or casserole. Pour off excess fat, add a little liquid (wine, water, stock, etc.) heat moderately, stirring and scraping. This then serves as a base for sauces.

feta a soft white cheese preserved in brine (salted water), originally made in Greece from sheep's milk.

ginger a gnarled root that needs to be peeled before it can be used, grated or chopped. It is now also available ready to use in little jars. Fresh ginger can be crystallised or preserved. Pickled in vinegar, it becomes a condiment known as *Gari*. Ginger is also sold ground as a powder.

harissa sold in jars or tubes, this very strong paste from the Middle East is made with chilli, garlic, spices and olive oil.

lemon curd made with lemons, butter, eggs and sugar, it is sold in jars and meant for spreading on bread.

lime has a sharper and more intense flavour than lemon and is used for marinades or making sauces.

Marinade an aromatic liquid made with spices, wine, soy sauce and so on, in which meat, fish or vegetables can be steeped in order to tenderise and flavour them.

Mascarpone an Italian cream cheese that is used to make tiramisu. It can also be sweetened and mixed with maple syrup, honey, etc. Often used as an accompaniment to strawberries and peaches.

Mozzarella this Italian cow's milk cheese is soft and runny, and can be eaten raw or cooked.

It is primarily marketed in a ball shape and comes preserved in whey or salt water in a watertight sachet. There is a superior quality mozzarella that is obtained from buffalo milk, which is less common and more expensive; it has a special flavour and a more distinctive texture.

Mustard there are many varieties, both plain and flavoured. One popular variety used in cooking is Dijon mustard from France. Mustard helps to bind cold ingredients, when making salad dressing or mayonnaise.

naan bread a round, flat bread from India or Pakistan.

nuoc mam this seasoning comes from Asia and is based on fermented dried fish.

nutella® this is made from chocolate, ground hazelnuts and milk by the company Ferrero, and is meant for spreading on slices of bread.

Peppers are very highly prized in Asian, Tex-Mex, and Hispanic cookery. Besides the familiar sweet peppers, the hot red and green chilli peppers come in different varieties and strengths, including 'scotch bonnet' and 'bird's-eye'.

pitta round, flat bread of Greek origin.

poach cook gently in liquid just below boiling point.

reduce leaving a sauce or gravy to cook until the liquid has evaporated enough to produce a thick consistency.

ricotta strained white cheese, originally from Italy, which is used to stuff vegetables, meat, etc.

Sear to seal the outside of meat briefly in very hot fat or on a hot, dry griddle pan to prevent the juices from escaping.

Shiitake brown Asian mushroom sold either fresh or dried.

Simmer cook very slowly, over a low heat.

Soy sauce made from fermented soya, it is widely used in Asia for flavouring dishes. It can be added to marinades and used for deglazing.

Stir-fry the traditional Chinese method of cooking in a metal wok over high heat

tahina sesame seed paste, which is mixed with puréed chickpeas to make hummus.

thyme aromatic plant used in Mediterranean cooking. Fresh or dried, it is used to flavour meat, fish, vegetables, pasta and so on.

tofu soya bean curd.

Vanilla originally from Central America, vanilla is the fruit of the vanilla plant. It comes in the form of a brown pod that can either be used whole or slit open to free the seeds that are inside. It can flavour desserts or the water for poaching white fish. Vanilla extract is made from vanilla.

Wasabi a Japanese plant that grows in streams. This green-coloured, very hot, spicy condiment, comes in powder or paste form and has a stronger flavour than horseradish. It is used to spice up raw fish and salads.

Wok a Chinese frying pan with a rounded base and deep sides that open out towards the top. Used for cooking, searing and frying quickly.

index of recipes

index of recipes to make in advance

photographic credits

Brasserie Thoumieux 79, rue Saint-Dominique, 75007 Paris, France © *Donald Van Der Putten* 29.

Getty Images *Leigh Beisch* 79 – *Benjamin F Fink Jr* 125 – *Alexandra Grablewski* 131 – *Simon Jauncey* 4 tr, 74 – *Paul Poplis* 71 – *Mark Thomas* 59 – *VCL* 13.

Nicolas Leser 148.

Option Photo *Philippe Asset* 30, 121 – *Dominique Azambre* 4 tl, 61 – *Franck Bel* 4 bl, 69 – *Belem* 4 br, 154 – *Bernard Felgeirolles* 73 – *Guy Félix* 49, 113, 132 – *Marquis* 93, 95.

Sucré Salé *Yves Bagros* 104 – *Pierre Desgrieux* 15 – *Pierre Hussenot* 87 – *Jean-Christophe Riou* 65.

Top *Frédéric Bouillard* 101 – *Jean-François Rivière* 135 – *Bernhard Winkelmann* 97.

Philippe Vaurès Santamaria: cover.

DR 48, 50, 56, 76, 84, 85, 114, 117, 136, 137, 146 –147.